P9-BIF-938

English in Context
Idioms

Betty Kirkpatrick MA

© 2001 Learners Publishing Pte Ltd

First published 2001 by
Learners Publishing Pte Ltd
222 Tagore Lane
#03-01 TG Building
Singapore 787603

Email: learnpub@learners.com.sg
Website: http://www.learners.com.sg

Reprinted 2001 (twice), 2002 (three times), 2003

All rights reserved. No part of this book shall be reproduced, or transmitted by any means, electronic or mechanical, including photocopying, recording, or by any information storage and retrieval system, without written permission from the publisher.

ISBN 981 4070 64 5

Printed by Press Ace Pte Ltd, Singapore

Please remember that unauthorized photocopying of this book is illegal.

Preface

The purpose of this *English in Context* series is, as the title indicates, to show students how various aspects of English, such as idioms and phrasal verbs, are actually used. The passages, which have been specially written for the series, bring to students a very clear idea of how these various aspects are used in context. The use of passages, rather than a single example sentence of the kind found in most dictionaries, demonstrates in a lively and graphic way just how words and sentences relate to each other and how English is actually put together.

Idioms play an important part in English and it is vital for students to understand them and to be able to use them. This is not easy, as idioms are phrases whose meanings cannot be understood from the meanings of the individual words which form them. They are metaphorical rather than literal. For example, the idiom **go to the wall** does not simply mean 'to walk over to a wall', but 'to become bankrupt or financially ruined'.

Each section of this text includes: a specially written passage containing ten idioms, a list of the idioms used, together with clear definitions and example sentences, and a set of questions to test how much knowledge students have gained from the passage and definitions.

The book demonstrates the extent and diversity of English idioms. Students who wish to speak or write English effectively and naturally must master them. They will find this book an invaluable aid to doing so.

Contents

Idioms
in Use

1 The Driving Test

Idioms in Context

Jenny was on her way to take her driving test and she was **a bundle of nerves**. Despite having got up at the **crack of dawn** to read her driving manual once more, she felt that she knew nothing. If only she had listened to her father. 'It's easier to get a job if you can drive,' he had said and offered to **foot the bill** for the lessons. 'I'll think about it,' Jenny had replied and **put** the idea **on the back burner** for some time. When she left college and started job-hunting, she discovered that her father had **hit the nail on the head**. There were indeed more jobs available for drivers. One of her friends was a sales rep for a publishing company and Jenny had **set her heart on** getting a similar job. That meant getting a driving licence. With a great deal of encouragement from family and friends she had **plucked up** enough **courage** to enrol for driving lessons. 'Learning to drive is **a piece of cake**,' Jenny's brother kept saying, but she found it quite difficult. Although her instructor, Mr Black, was sure that she would pass **with flying colours** at her first attempt, she herself was not so confident. However, Mr Black was right. As Jenny came out of the test centre to meet her family, she was **grinning from ear to ear**. She had passed. Now she would be able to apply for the job — and get a company car.

Know the Meaning

be a bundle of nerves

to be very nervous: *Jill is always a bundle of nerves when she has to sit an exam.*

at crack of dawn

very early in the morning: *We'll have to leave home at crack of dawn to catch the first bus.*

foot the bill

to pay (for something): *Jack applied for a bank loan to help him foot the bill for his daughter's wedding.*

put *(something)* **on the back burner**

to delay dealing with (something), to set (something) aside in order to attend to it later: *Their plans to move house have been put on the back burner for the moment.*

hit the nail on the head

to be absolutely accurate or exact: *My father hit the nail on the head when he said that Jack was a villain.*

set one's heart on *(something)*

to be very keen to get or do (something), to want (something) very much: *Jan has set her heart on studying medicine. The child had set his heart on a trip to the seaside.*

pluck up courage/screw up one's courage

to force oneself to do something, although one might be feeling afraid or unwilling: *The junior clerk finally plucked up courage and asked his boss for a wage rise.*

a piece of cake *(informal)*

something very easy or simple to do: *The first exam was a piece of cake but the others were very difficult.*

with flying colours

very easily and successfully: *Anne came through the job interview with flying colours.*

grin from ear to ear

to smile broadly, to look very pleased or happy: *The coach of the local football team was grinning from ear to ear when they won the cup.*

Do it Yourself

1 If you were described as being **a bundle of nerves** would you be feeling calm and confident?

2 If you get up **at crack of dawn** are you a late riser?

3 Fill in an idiom to complete the sentence:

Luke was surprised that he was left to _____ in the restaurant — he had thought that they were going to divide it among them.

4 If you **put something on the back burner** do you attend to it immediately?

5 If you **hit the nail on the head** are you accurate?

6 If you have **set your heart on something** are you reluctant to have it?

7 Give an idiom that is very similar in form to **pluck up one's courage** and means exactly the same.

8 Give an idiom which you could use to say that something is very easy.

9 If students very nearly fail an exam would you say that they had passed **with flying colours?**

10 Give an idiom which has the same meaning as **grin from ear to ear**.

2 Avoiding Party Preparations

Idioms in Context

Bill could hear his mother calling him but he **turned a deaf ear**. She was giving a large dinner party that evening and it needed a great deal of organization. The whole household was **at sixes and sevens**. Having spent the morning cleaning the windows, mowing the lawn and moving chairs around, Bill was **all in**. A few minutes ago he had made for the garden shed to have a rest and read the newspaper, saying to himself, 'It's time to **lie low** for a while.' Suddenly the shed door opened. Bill looked up to see his brother Rob standing there. 'This is where you are,' Rob said. 'You're really **in** mum's **bad books**. She wanted you to collect the meat from the butcher's.' 'What are you doing here?' asked Bill. 'Mum's **turning** the house **upside down** looking for a recipe,' said Rob. 'Apparently she wrote it on a piece of paper and left it on the hall table. I decided to **make myself scarce** until she calms down. Dad's helping her look for it.' Rob had just sat down beside Bill when their father appeared. 'So this is where you're hiding,' he said. 'You'll both be **in hot water** when your mother finds you. She's **like a cat on hot bricks** about this party and says that there's no one to help her. She's going to the hairdresser in a few minutes and I'm staying here until **the coast is clear**.'

Know the Meaning

turn a deaf ear to (something)

to refuse to listen to or pay attention to (something): *The workers pleaded with the boss to give them more money but he turned a deaf ear to their request.*

at sixes and sevens

in confusion, in a muddle, in a disorganized state: *The students are all going home today and the place is at sixes and sevens.*

all in

exhausted, very tired: *I can't reach the top of the hill — I'm all in.*

lie low

to stay quiet or hidden, to avoid drawing attention to oneself: *The police think that the bank robbers are lying low somewhere. Their mother was in a bad mood and so the children were lying low.*

in (someone's) **bad books/in** (someone's) **black books**

unpopular with (someone), out of favour with (someone): *I damaged dad's car and I'm now in his bad books.*

turn (somewhere) **upside down**

to cause confusion and mess (somewhere), usually when looking thoroughly for something: *The police turned the students' flat upside down looking for drugs. I've turned the place upside down and I can't find my ring.*

make oneself scarce

to get out of the way quickly, usually to avoid trouble or difficulty: *The students were demonstrating against high fees but they made themselves scarce when the police arrived.*

in hot water

in trouble: *You'll be in hot water if you're late for work again.*

like a cat on hot bricks

very nervous and restless: *Jane has been like a cat on hot bricks all morning waiting for her exam results.*

the coast is clear

there is no longer any danger or difficulty present: *The burglars watched everyone leave the building and broke in when the coast was clear.*

Do it Yourself

1 If you **turn a deaf ear to** someone's instructions do you listen to these carefully?

2 If a kitchen is **at sixes and sevens** does it look neat and tidy?

3 How are you feeling if you describe yourself as being **all in**?

4 Write the missing word to complete the idiom:

   *The robbers are **lying** _____ while the police are looking for them.*

5 Give an idiom which is opposite in meaning to **in (someone's) bad books**.

6 Under what circumstances would you be likely to **turn somewhere upside down**?

7 Replace the underlined words with an idiom:

   It's time to get out quickly — my brother has discovered that I got a stain on his best silk tie.

8 Give an idiom which means 'in trouble'.

9 Write the missing word to complete the idiom:

   *If someone is very nervous and restless you would say that they are **like a cat on** _____ **bricks**.*

10 Would you feel safe to proceed if **the coast is clear**?

3 Saving a Business

Idioms in Context

Peter was looking **down in the mouth**. He had just opened a statement from the bank and his account was **in the red**. This was really bad news as he had recently started a new computer business and it was having a few **teething troubles**. It always takes quite a long time to **get** a new company **off the ground** and, although Peter had a great many customers, he was finding that they did not always pay promptly. Without more money coming in, the young man was worried that his business might soon **go to the wall**. He had no competitors in the town and was convinced that he would make a profit **in the long run**. However, he needed time — and money. Over the years he had borrowed a great deal of money from his parents and he knew that his father would **hit the roof** if he asked for more. Peter already had a small loan from the bank but he was going to have to try to increase this in order to stay in business. It would not be easy as the banks were not being particularly generous at the moment, but he had no other choice. All the way to the bank Peter was **on tenterhooks** but, when the bank manager looked at Peter's business plan and saw that everything was **above board**, he agreed to help. The loan was not large but, if Peter **tightened his belt**, his business would be safe for some time.

Know the Meaning

down in the mouth

miserable or depressed: *Sara seems rather down in the mouth — did she fail the English test?*

in the red

in debt, (of a bank account) overdrawn: *May is highly paid and yet her account's in the red at the end of every month.*

teething troubles

problems or difficulties which occur at the start of something: *The builders had a few teething troubles with our new office block but they finished it on schedule.*

get *(something)* **off the ground**

to get (something) started and operating successfully: *We're trying to start a new tennis club but we'll never get it off the ground without more members.*

go to the wall

to fail, to be financially unsuccessful, to go bankrupt: *Sales of the new product were poor and the company went to the wall.*

in the long run

eventually, in the end, after a long period of time: *It is hard having no money as a student but studying is worth it in the long run — you will get a better-paid job.*

hit the roof

to become extremely angry: *Mother will hit the roof when she sees the stain on the new carpet.*

on tenterhooks

uncertain and extremely tense and nervous about what is going to happen: *The exam results were to be announced soon and the students were on tenterhooks.*

above board

open and honest, without hiding anything: *I would check whether Jack's business is above board before investing any money in it.*

tighten one's belt

to economize greatly, to spend a great deal less money: *Joe and Sue have just had another child and have had to tighten their belts.*

Do it Yourself

1 If you were **down in the mouth** would you be smiling?

2 Give a phrase which means the opposite of **in the red**.

3 Do **teething troubles** occur at the beginning or end of something?

4 Write down an idiom which means the same as **get (something) up and running**.

5 Replace the underlined word with an idiom:

The firm is losing sales and the workers are afraid that it will <u>fail</u>.

6 If workers are going to be promoted **in the long run** will their promotion happen very soon?

7 Replace the idiom with another idiom of similar meaning:

*Dad will **hit the roof** if you borrow his car without permission.*

8 If you are **on tenterhooks** are you calm or nervous?

9 Would you trust someone who was not **above board**?

10 Write down an idiom which is similar in meaning to **tighten one's belt**.

4 What to Wear?

Idioms in Context

It was Saturday night and Meg should have been getting ready for a party. This was to celebrate her friend Joan's twenty-first birthday, but Meg was **in two minds about** going. The problem was clothes. She knew that all the guests would be **dressed to the nines** and she had not been able to afford to buy a new dress. Being a student, she was **living on a shoestring** and all her money went on rent, food and books. Now it was the end of term and she did **not have a penny to her name**. Still, Joan would be offended if she did not appear at the party and so **there was nothing else for it**. She would just have to wear the dress that she had worn to all the other parties this term, even though it was **falling to bits**. Just as Meg was ironing the dress Carol came rushing into the room. She shared a flat with Meg and, although they were not related, the two girls **looked like two peas in a pod**. 'Why don't you borrow a dress from me?' cried Carol. She had a huge wardrobe full of clothes given to her by her father who was **rolling in money**. 'That gold-coloured one will **suit you down to the ground**.' Meg was reluctant to accept but eventually agreed to borrow the dress and was the **belle of the ball** when she arrived at the party.

Know the Meaning

be in two minds about (*something*)

to be unable to come to a decision about (something): *Fred has been offered a job but it is out of town and he is in two minds about accepting it.*

be dressed to the nines

to be dressed in formal, smart clothes, sometimes over-dressed: *Jane usually wears jeans and a sweater and hates parties where everyone is dressed to the nines.*

be living on a shoestring

to have very little money to live on: *The young mother is living on a shoestring and cannot afford to buy sweets for her children.*

not to have a penny to one's name

to be extremely poor: *The groom is very rich but the bride doesn't have a penny to her name.*

there is nothing else for it

there is only one thing to do, there is no choice: *When Mark's car broke down several miles from the town there was nothing else for it — he had to walk.*

be falling to bits

to be in a very bad state of repair, to be torn or broken: *Jack tried to sell me a car but you could see that it was falling to bits.*

look like two peas in a pod

to look very much alike: *The two girls must be sisters — they look like two peas in a pod.*

be rolling in money (*informal*)

to have a great deal of money, to be very rich: *You would have to be rolling in money to be able to afford a house in that part of town. Mark's dad's rolling in money but he won't give him a loan.*

suit (*someone*) **down to the ground**

to suit (someone) extremely well, to be exactly right for (someone): *Jim loves travelling and so that job will suit him down to the ground.*

belle of the ball

the most attractive woman or girl present at a gathering: *There were many beautiful women at the party but everyone agreed that Vicky was the belle of the ball.*

Do it Yourself

1 If you are **in two minds about** whether to go somewhere or not have you come to a decision yet?

2 If your friends are wearing their old, casual clothes would you say that they are **dressed to the nines?**

3 Write the missing word to complete the idiom:

   *After he was declared redundant the family had to **live on a** _____.*

4 When there is **nothing else for it** how many choices do you have?

5 If you do **not have a penny to your name** can you afford to lend someone money?

6 If curtains are **falling to bits** are they in a good state of repair?

7 Replace the underlined words with an idiom from the passage:

   The two little girls looked very <u>like each other</u>.

8 Would you describe a very poor person as **rolling in money?**

9 Replace the idiom with one of similar meaning:

   *Mike loves working outdoors — a job as a gardener will **suit him down to the ground**.*

10 Would you describe a plain, badly-dressed young woman as the **belle of the ball?**

5 A Proposal of Marriage

Idioms in Context

Jane was **in seventh heaven**. Jack had just **popped the question** and she had said yes. They wanted to get married as soon as possible, but knew that Jane's parents would want to **spare no expense** for their only daughter's wedding. Organizing this could take a long time and both Jane and Jack would have preferred an informal occasion. Still, Jane **thought the world of** her family and would agree to a large wedding if they wanted one. The young couple were hoping to **keep** their engagement **under wraps** until they could tell both sets of parents in person next day. However, they were smiling so happily that their friends guessed that they had some good news and asked what it was. Eventually Jane's best friend, Mary, made her **come clean** and everyone congratulated the happy couple. They begged their friends not to tell anyone else but Mary **let the cat out of the bag** and the news spread rapidly round the town. By the time Jane and Jack arrived for lunch next day both sets of parents were already **in the know**. Realizing that the young people would want to tell them of their engagement themselves, the parents pretended to know nothing about it. Since Jane and Jack had been dating for some time, both families had suspected that an engagement was **on the cards**. Now that it had actually been announced, they all looked forward to the happy day when the couple would **tie the knot**.

Know the Meaning

in seventh heaven

extremely happy or pleased, delighted: *The young mother was in seventh heaven when she held her newborn baby.*

pop the question *(informal)*

to ask someone to marry you, to propose to someone: *Mary is longing to get married and hopes that her boyfriend will pop the question soon.*

spare no expense

to spend whatever sum of money it takes to get what one wants without worrying about the cost of this: *Our neighbours spared no expense on their anniversary party — they had several crates of the best vintage champagne.*

think the world of *(someone)*

to be very fond of (someone): *Jill thought the world of her daughter-in-law and was very upset when her son divorced her.*

keep *(something)* under wraps

to keep (something) secret: *The firm is keeping its new product under wraps until the official launch.*

come clean

to tell the truth about something, especially to admit that you have done something wrong, to confess: *You might as well come clean — our neighbour saw you break the window.*

let the cat out of the bag

to reveal a secret, often unintentionally: *We had planned a surprise party for our parents' wedding anniversary but my sister let the cat out of the bag.*

in the know

having information known only to a small group of people: *Only those in the know had any idea that George was going to a new job.*

on the cards

very likely to happen: *Some of the staff know that the closure of the firm is on the cards and are looking for other jobs.*

tie the knot

to get married: *Liz and Bill are going to tie the knot in the local registry office, not in church.*

Do it Yourself

1 Replace the idiom with an idiom of similar meaning:

*The children were **in seventh heaven** when they were told of the party.*

2 Write the missing word to complete the idiom:

*When a man asks a woman to marry him we say that he has **popped the** _____ .*

3 If you spare no expense are you being careful with your money?

4 Write down an idiom which is similar in meaning to **think that there is no one like (someone)**.

5 If you **keep something under wraps** do you tell everyone about it?

6 If you **come clean** do you deny that you have done something wrong?

7 Replace the idiom with an idiom of similar meaning:

*The children were hiding from their mother in a cupboard but the youngest one **let the cat out of the bag** by sneezing.*

8 If facts are known by those who are **in the know** are they widely known?

9 If something is **on the cards** is it likely to happen?

10 Write down an informal idiom meaning the same as the idiom **tie the knot**.

6 Mother's Ban on Motorbikes

Idioms in Context

'You are not buying a motorbike and **that's flat**,' shouted Mrs Grey angrily and left the room. Her son. Tim, looked hopefully at his father but he said, 'I'm not **taking sides** in this argument. It's between you and your mother.' 'But dad,' replied Tim, 'you had a motorbike when you were young and you used to say that you loved going **like the wind**. I've saved up the money and I don't understand why I can't have one if you had one.' 'That was **a different kettle of fish**,' said Mr Grey. 'When I was your age there was much less traffic on the roads and there were not so many accidents. Besides, your mother would be **worried sick** if you were out driving a motorbike. She thinks you'd be **dicing with death**.' 'But I'd be careful,' argued Tim. 'Most of the bikers who get killed or injured **risk their necks** by not taking any safety precautions. I would **play safe** and wear a protective helmet and I wouldn't speed.' 'Tim, I told you, I'm not getting involved in this argument and I'm tired of hearing you and your mother **going at it hammer and tongs**. There's no point in going on asking for a motorbike. Your mother has **dug her heels in**. You should put the money towards a small car and we'll lend you the rest.' Tim went away to think about this, still muttering about motorbikes.

Know the Meaning

that's flat

that is final, there is to be no more discussion or argument: *I'm not lending you my car and that's flat!*

take sides

to support a particular person, group, etc against another, not to remain neutral: *Jim and his twin sister are always arguing but their elder brother refuses to take sides.*

like the wind

very quickly: *The child ran like the wind to tell his mother the good news.*

a different kettle of fish

something completely different: *I quite like singing around the house, but singing in public is a different kettle of fish.*

worried sick

extremely anxious and worried: *The family on the beach can't find their little girl and they are worried sick.*

dice with death (sometimes used humorously)

to risk putting oneself in great danger or getting into serious trouble: *Those racing drivers look as though they're dicing with death. I'll be dicing with death if I ask my father for another loan.*

risk their necks

to take a serious risk, to risk putting oneself in danger or getting into serious trouble: *You shouldn't have risked your neck going back into the burning house to get your jewellery. Pete risked his neck by asking the boss not to sack Bill for being late.*

play safe/play it safe

to act with care and caution, not to take risks: *It doesn't look as though it will rain, but I'm going to play it safe and take an umbrella.*

go at it hammer and tongs

to have a fierce argument or row: *We had a dreadful journey — Anne and Bert were going at it hammer and tongs all the time about who was the better driver.*

dig in one's heels/dig one's heels in

stubbornly to refuse to agree to something, allow something, etc: *We hoped to persuade Judy to change her mind when she refused to join us, but she dug her heels in.*

Do it Yourself

1 Would you use the idiom **that's flat** if you had any doubts about what you were saying?

2 If you **take sides** in an argument do you remain neutral?

3 Write down an idiom which means *very slowly*.

4 If you find yourself **in a whole new ball game** are you in a familiar situation or in a completely different one?

5 Replace the underlined words with an idiom:

Amy is <u>very anxious and worried</u> because she has lost her job and cannot afford to pay the rent.

6 Write the missing word to complete the idiom:

*You'll be **dicing with** _____ if you drive that old car.*

7 Write the missing word to complete the idiom:

*Get out of the burning house now. Don't **risk your** _____!*

8 If you tend to **play it safe** are you likely to be a reckless person?

9 Write down an idiom which is similar in meaning to **go at it hammer and tongs**.

10 If you **dig in your heels** do you meekly agree to do something?

7 Amy's Holiday Problem

Idioms in Context

Amy and her boyfriend Andrew had just finished their second year at college and were supposed to be celebrating. 'Come on, it's time to **let our hair down** after all that studying,' cried Amy. 'Wait a minute,' said Andrew. I wanted to talk about our holiday. How would you like to go backpacking with me in Europe?' 'My father would **have a fit** if I even suggested it,' replied Amy. 'You know how strict he is.' 'But we've been **going out with** each other for more than a year now,' said Andrew. Why don't I ask him if it would be all right?' 'I wouldn't **cross swords with** my father if I were you,' Amy commented. 'He's only just got used to my having a boyfriend. It would be silly to **make waves**. It would be better to talk to my mother first. She **has** dad **wrapped round** her **little finger**.' 'Can we talk to her soon,' asked Andrew. 'I'd like to get the holiday organized as soon as possible.' 'There's no point in **rushing our fences**,' Amy objected. 'It would be better to sort out our plans first before we approach mum. She's much more likely to talk to dad if she thinks we've **got** the whole thing **taped** and we know what we're doing. If she thinks we've **bitten off more than we can chew** she'll say no.' 'All right,' agreed Andrew. 'Let's get the guidebooks out. We can **paint the town** another night.'

Know the Meaning

let one's hair down

to relax and enjoy oneself: *Our boss is always very formal in the office but she really lets her hair down at parties.*

have a fit *(informal)*

to become very angry: *Mr Smith will have a fit if he sees that dog digging up his garden.*

go out with *(someone)*

to date (someone) on a regular basis: *Matt and Libby have been going out with each other for several years but they have no plans to get married.*

cross swords with *(someone)*

to quarrel with (someone), to have a disagreement with (someone): *The president of the club is not used to people disagreeing with him but the new member has crossed swords with him over certain rules.*

make waves

to cause trouble: *This was a very peaceful place to work until Tom arrived — he's always making waves.*

have *(someone)* **wrapped/wound/twisted round one's little finger**

to be able to persuade (someone) to act exactly as one wishes: *If we all want more time to finish the essay we should get Emma to ask the teacher — she has him wrapped round her little finger.*

rush one's fences

to act with too much hurry and not enough care: *Jerry was rushing his fences by asking Pam to marry him a month after they met.*

have *(something)* **taped**

to have a full knowledge and understanding of (something): *My grandfather had difficulty learning to use a computer at first, but he seems to have got it taped now.*

bite off more than one can chew

to try to cope with more than one is capable of or to try to do something that is too difficult: *Mary had bitten off more than she could chew when she went back to work full-time shortly after she had twins.*

paint the town/paint the town red

celebrate by going out to enjoy oneself in an extravagant, often noisy manner: *When the local football team won the cup all the fans decided to paint the town red.*

Do it Yourself

1 Write down an idiom which is similar in meaning to **have a fit**.

2 If people are **letting their hair down** are they working hard?

3 Replace the idiom with an idiom of similar meaning:

*Sue has a new boyfriend — she stopped **going out with** Mike last month.*

4 If you **cross swords with someone** are you being friendly?

5 If people like to **make waves** are they usually peace-makers?

6 Fill in an idiom to complete the sentence:

The Smith's youngest daughter has her grandfather _____.

7 Write down an idiom which is opposite in meaning to **rush one's fences**.

8 If you are ignorant about something could you say that you **have it taped**?

9 If you **bite off more than you can chew** can you cope with what you are trying to do?

10 Write down an idiom which is similar in meaning to **paint the town red**.

8 Finding a Flat-mate

Idioms in Context

Philip and Kenny were discussing their plans to share a flat. They had found one which **fitted the bill** perfectly, but the rent was rather expensive for just two of them. 'There's enough room for three. Why don't we ask Ben to share with us?' asked Philip. 'I'd join you **like a shot**,' said Ben when asked, 'but I'm **as poor as a church mouse** at the moment.' 'We don't have to pay anything until we move in at the start of next term. You could get a job and save up over the summer,' suggested Kenny. 'Well-paid student jobs are **like gold dust** but I'll see what I can find,' replied Ben. Philip and Kenny hoped that their friend would **get a move on** and let them know soon if he could afford to join them. **At a pinch** they could afford the flat without a third person, but they would have to **live from hand to mouth**. They were both confident that Ben would make an ideal flat-mate. When they first met him he was a bit unreliable but he had **turned over a new leaf** after failing his first-term exams. Now they were **hoping against hope** that he would find a job to pay the advance rent and the deposit. When he called that evening to say that he had got a job as a gardener for the summer it was **a load off their minds**. They quickly rang the landlord to accept the flat.

Know the Meaning

fit the bill
to be exactly what is required, to be extremely suitable: *I've been looking for a birthday present for my sister and this watch will fill the bill.*

like a shot
very willingly or eagerly: *I would go on holiday with you like a shot but I've arranged to go away with my family then.*

as poor as a church mouse
very poor, having very little money: *He's a wealthy surgeon now but he was as poor as a church mouse when he was a medical student.*

like gold dust
extremely rare: *The band is very popular and tickets for tonight's concert are like gold dust.*

get a move on *(informal)*
to move more quickly, to hurry: *If we don't get a move on we'll not be able to complete the project.*

at a pinch
if it becomes absolutely necessary, in an emergency: *At a pinch we could get four people in the back seat of the car, but it would be uncomfortable.*

live from hand to mouth
to have enough money to supply only what is really needed for survival, to be very poor: *Both parents are unemployed and the family are living from hand to mouth.*

turn over a new leaf
to begin to behave well after a period of bad behaviour: *The child was very badly behaved in school at first but after a few weeks he has turned over a new leaf.*

hope against hope
to go on hoping that something will happen when there is no reason to believe that it will: *The family were hoping against hope that the emergency operation on their mother would be successful.*

be a load/weight off one's mind
to be a relief from something that has been worrying one: *Josh had taken out a bank loan as a student and it was a load off his mind when he was able to pay it off.*

Do it Yourself

1 Replace the underlined words with an idiom:

I know you're looking for a new secretary but I can't think of anyone who <u>is exactly what you require</u>.

2 If you did something **like a shot** would you be unwilling to do it?

3 Write the missing word to complete the idiom:

*The old man is **as poor as a** _____ **mouse**.*

4 If something is **like gold dust** would you find it easily?

5 Write down two informal idioms which are similar in meaning to **get a move on**.

6 Write the missing word to complete the idiom:

***At a** _____ we could seat eight people round the dining-room table.*

7 If you live **from hand to mouth** are you likely to be able to save for a holiday?

8 If people **turn over a new leaf** do they change for the better?

9 Fill in an idiom to complete the sentence:

The patient was very badly injured but the doctors are _____ that he will survive.

10 Write down an idiom which is very similar both in meaning and in form to **take a load off one's mind**.

9 Night Fears

'What a terrifying film!' exclaimed Patsy. Her friend Mel was staying the night at her house and they were both **shaking in their shoes** after watching a ghost film about a woman being murdered in a graveyard. 'It **scared** me **out of** my **wits**. I wish we weren't going to be alone in the house,' said Mel. Patsy's brother, Donald, had offered to come and stay while their parents were away but, if she had accepted, he would have teased the girls about not **having the bottle to** sleep in the house alone. 'It was only a film,' said Patsy. 'Let's go up to bed.' She was **putting on a brave face** to make Mel feel better. Upstairs with all the lights on, they felt a bit better. Although Mel would have liked to ask to share Patsy's room, she decided to **bite the bullet** and sleep in the spare room. 'It's time to **hit the hay** — I'm exhausted!' yawned Patsy. So saying she climbed into bed and was soon **dead to the world**. Despite her nerves, Mel soon **followed suit**. But not for long. Suddenly she heard a creaking sound that **made** her **blood run cold**. Then there was a ghostly shriek. 'Patsy!' she screamed, leaping out of bed. Patsy **had her heart in her mouth** when she arrived. Then she saw the wardrobe door opening and a small shape appear. She laughed and said, 'It's OK. It's only the cat from next door! She's had kittens in the wardrobe!'

 **Know the Meaning**

shake in one's shoes

to be very nervous or scared: *We were shaking in our shoes when the policeman started to question us.*

scare/frighten *(someone)* **out of** *(his/her)* **wits**

to frighten (someone) very much: *We were frightened out of our wits when we heard the strange noise coming from the graveyard.*

have the bottle to *(do something)*

to be brave or bold enough (to do something), to have the courage (to do something): *It took a lot of bottle to admit in public that he had made a mistake.*

put a brave face on it/put on a brave face

to try to appear calm, confident, happy, etc when one has no cause to feel like this: *Rose was very disappointed at losing the tennis match but she put a brave face on it as she left the court.*

bite the bullet

to deal as bravely as possible with something that is unpleasant but unavoidable: *The boss valued all of his workforce, but the firm had cash problems and he had to bite the bullet and declare some of them redundant.*

hit the hay/sack *(informal)*

to go to bed: *I'm going to hit the hay — I've got to get up early in the morning.*

be dead to the world

to be deeply asleep: *I thought that I heard the baby cry but he was dead to the world.*

follow suit

to do what someone else has just done: *Jack left the room and his friends followed suit.*

make *(someone's)* **blood run cold**

to make (someone) feel extremely frightened or horrified: *My blood ran cold as I heard the heavy footsteps behind me in the dark alley.*

have one's heart in one's mouth

to be very anxious and nervous: *We had our hearts in our mouths as the ghostly shape came towards us.*

 **Do it Yourself**

1 How are you feeling if you **are shaking in your shoes**?

2 Write the missing word to complete the idiom:

*We were **scared out of** our _____ when the old man threatened us.*

3 Write down an idiom which is opposite in meaning to **have the bottle to do something**.

4 Write the missing word to complete the idiom:

*Beth had to **put a brave _____ on it** when her boyfriend went off with another girl.*

5 Is **biting the bullet** a cowardly action?

6 What time of day do you usually **hit the hay**?

7 Replace the underlined words with an idiom from the passage above:

The children went straight to bed and are <u>fast asleep</u> now.

8 If you **follow suit** do you do the same as someone else?

9 Write the missing word to complete the idiom:

*The boy's _____ **ran cold** when he saw the knife in his attacker's hand.*

10 If you **have your heart in your mouth** are you feeling very brave and confident?

10 A Student Joke

Idioms in Context

Usually Rob strolled along, but today he was racing past **like a bat out of hell**. He simply had to get to the college library before it closed for the weekend. 'I'll really be **burning the midnight oil** tonight,' he thought as he hurried on. Rob's English class had been told to write an essay on the English novelist Charles Dickens and he **didn't have a clue about** him. He was hoping that he'd find some books to **point** him **in the right direction**. Rob was not a Dickens fan. Indeed he found the writer **as dull as ditchwater**. Still, the essay would have to be written. Up till a few minutes ago Rob had thought that he was **sitting pretty** as far as the English essay was concerned. According to his diary the essay was not due for three weeks. However, some of his fellow students had just told him that the date had been brought forward to Monday. Rob was **in a cold sweat**. However, he reached the library **in the nick of time** and got the books. What surprised him was that he didn't see any of his friends there. Why weren't they getting books for the essay? Suddenly he saw them standing in a group at the coffee shop and they were **laughing their heads off**. 'The essay hasn't been brought forward at all. We were just **taking the mickey out of** you,' they said. Rob was so relieved that he laughed too.

Know the Meaning

like a bat out of hell

extremely quickly, very fast: *When the burglars heard the police car siren he ran out the back of the building like a bat out of hell.*

burn the midnight oil

to study or work until very late at night: *I'll be burning the midnight oil from now until the exams.*

not to have a clue about (something)

to know nothing or very little about (something), to be ignorant about (something): *Jeff is brilliant at English and history but he doesn't have a clue about maths.*

point (someone) **in the right direction**

to show (someone) what to do, to help (someone) get started on (something): *Tom's father wants to buy a computer but he knows very little about them — he's hoping that Tom will point him in the right direction.*

as dull as ditchwater

extremely dull or uninteresting: *The lecture was as dull as ditchwater and so we left early.*

be sitting pretty

to be in a fortunate or favourable situation: *The local football team is sitting pretty at the top of the league.*

be in a cold sweat

to be in a state of fear and anxiety: *The girls were in a cold sweat waiting to see if the last bus had gone.*

in the nick of time

at the last possible moment, just before it is too late: *The ambulance got there in the nick of time — the accident victim nearly died.*

laugh one's head off

to laugh loudly or heartily: *Mark laughed his head off when his rival fell off his bike.*

take the mickey out of (someone)

to make fun of (someone), to tease (someone), to ridicule (someone): *The new teacher is very inexperienced and the students are always taking the mickey out of him.*

Do it Yourself

1 If you were moving **like a bat out of hell** would you be crawling along?

2 If you regularly **burn the midnight oil** do you usually go to bed early?

3 Do you know a great deal about something if you **do not have a clue about** it?

4 If people **point** you **in the right direction** are they helping or hindering you?

5 Write the missing word to complete the idiom:

   This novel is as _____ as ditchwater.

6 If you are **sitting pretty** are you in trouble?

7 If you are **in a cold sweat** how are you feeling?

8 If you arrive **in the nick of time** have you got there early with plenty of time to spare?

9 Give an idiom which is opposite in meaning to **cry one's eyes out**.

10 Write the missing word to complete the idiom:

   *George's car hadn't really been stolen — his friends were **taking the _____ out of** him.*

11 The End of the Affair

Idioms in Context

Miriam wasn't feeling very happy. She and her fiancé, Tim, had just decided that they had **reached the parting of the ways**. Recently they seemed to have been constantly quarrelling. Tim would **pick a fight with** her and a violent argument would follow. Until today they had always ended their quarrel by **burying the hatchet** and going out for a romantic evening. Today, however, they had both realized that their relationship had not just **struck a bad patch**, but was coming to an end. Up till now, although both of them realized that their relationship had many problems, they had **papered over the cracks**, and gone on with their engagement. Yesterday they had quarrelled badly and last night Miriam had suggested meeting this morning to have a talk and try to **clear the air**. Sadly, after some discussion, they had decided that they were not going to be able to **patch up their differences** this time and that the best thing was to **call it a day**. Miriam decided to go and tell her parents, who had always liked Tim and who would be upset. On her way there she met Val and told her that she and Tim had **come to the end of the road**. Val was a very optimistic person and, instead of sympathizing, said cheerfully, 'Never mind. **There's plenty more fish in the sea**!' 'How I hate that expression!' thought Miriam, knowing she would hear it many times again.

Know the Meaning

reach the parting of the ways

to end a relationship or association: *Millie and Jane have been business partners for several years, but they have reached the parting of the ways and they are both starting their own firms.*

pick a fight with *(someone)*

to start a quarrel deliberately with (someone): *It's best to avoid Rob when he's been drinking — he usually picks a fight with someone.*

bury the hatchet

to agree to stop quarrelling or fighting and be friends again: *The Thomsons often quarrelled with their neighbours, but they buried the hatchet when their daughter started going out with their neighbour's son.*

strike a bad patch

to experience a period of difficulty in which there are many problems: *The computing firm struck a bad patch, but it is now very successful.*

paper over the cracks

to pretend that everything is all right when this is not the case: *Meg and Terry have separated after years of quarrelling although they tried to paper over the cracks for the sake of their children.*

clear the air

to make a situation less tense and difficult by talking about any problems: *There was a lot of confusion about who was responsible for what but we had a staff meeting to clear the air.*

patch up differences

to end an argument or quarrel by trying to forget about or ignore what caused it in order to remain friendly: *Margo and Billy are always arguing but they agreed to patch up their differences.*

call it a day

to decide or declare that something has come to an end: *Dad has been working at the same firm for thirty years but he has decided to call it a day and do something else.*

come to/reach the end of the road

to reach the end of some kind of relationship or association: *Matt and Rickie had been good friends, but their friendship came to the end of the road when Rickie asked his girlfriend out on a date.*

there are plenty more fish in the sea

a saying often used to someone who has just ended a relationship to reassure him/her that there are many more women/men in the world who could be potential partners: *Don't cry because Paul's left you — he wasn't really your type and there are plenty more fish in the sea.*

Do it Yourself

1 If two business partners **reach the parting of the ways** do they go on running the business together?

2 If you **pick a fight with** people do you want to quarrel with them?

3 Write the missing word to complete the idiom:
*Kim and Roy had a serious quarrel but they have decided to **bury the** _____.*

4 Write the missing word to complete the idiom:
*The hockey team was playing very well but it now seems to have **struck a bad** _____.*

5 If people **paper over the cracks** in their relationship do they openly admit that they are having problems?

6 Fill in an idiom to complete the sentence:
The neighbours were obviously feeling annoyed about the parking problems caused by the new pub and so the pub owner called a meeting to try to _____.

7 If you **patch up your differences with** someone do you go on quarrelling?

8 Fill in an idiom to complete the sentence:
The business is losing money and the owners have decided to _____ and close the shop.

9 Fill in an idiom to complete the sentence:
Tom and Sheila have decided that their marriage has _____ and have decided to get a divorce.

10 Write down a saying that is similar in meaning to **there are plenty more fish in the sea**.

12 Getting the Girl

Idioms in Context

'Just look at Pete! He's certainly **taken a shine to** the new girl in our class. He keeps looking at her,' said Jock as he joined a group of students for coffee after the English lecture. 'Don't be so shy, Pete! Why don't you **take the bull by the horns** and ask her to go to the cinema or something?' asked Angie as Pete came over to their table and sat down. 'I'd love to,' replied Pete, 'but I'm **not in the same league as** she is. She's so attractive and smartly dressed.' 'You're not exactly ugly yourself.' Beryl said. 'Go on! Ask her!' 'I'm scared that she'd **give** me **the brush-off**,' admitted Pete. 'A girl like that probably **wouldn't touch** me **with a bargepole**.' 'I'm beginning to **have a soft spot for** her myself. In fact she's just my kind of girl,' Jock said suddenly. 'If you don't ask her out, I will.' 'That's not fair. Now you're **twisting** my **arm**,' said Pete. 'Well, get on with it!' replied Jock. 'I think I will **take the plunge**.' said Pete. 'I don't want you **selling** me **down the river** and getting a date with her.' Having said that, Pete walked over to the table at which the new student, whose name was Selina, was sitting. 'It looks as though everything's going **like clockwork**,' said Meg as she watched Pete talking to Selina. Indeed it was. Selina had just agreed to go to the cinema with Pete on Saturday evening.

Know the Meaning

take a shine to *(someone/something) (informal)*

to become fond of (someone or something): *I think that Bert has taken a shine to Julie — he keeps looking at her.*

take the bull by the horns

to deal with something boldly and without delay: *Many of the staff were worried about being made redundant and so they decided to take the bull by the horns and ask for a meeting with the manager.*

be not in the same league as *(someone)*

to be not as good at something as (someone), or not as important as (someone): *Miriam is quite a good violinist, but she is not in the same league as her sister who plays with one of the national orchestras.*

give *(someone)* **the brush-off**

to treat someone in an unwelcoming way in order to get rid of him/her, to reject (someone) abruptly: *I applied for a job with a bank but I got a letter back immediately giving me the brush-off.*

not touch *(someone/something)* **with a bargepole**

to refuse to have any contact or involvement with someone or something: *I wouldn't touch that firm with a bargepole — the management treats the staff very badly.*

have a soft spot for *(someone/something)*

to be fond of (someone or something): *Edith's always had a soft spot for spaniels.*

twist *(someone's)* **arm**

to try to persuade (someone) to do something against his/her will, to put pressure on (someone) to do something: *Ellie seems reluctant to go to the party but, if you twist his arm, she'll probably go with you.*

take the plunge

to take decisive action, although this may be risky, especially after some hesitation: *Frank has been thinking of getting married for years and now he's taken the plunge and asked Peggy to be his wife.*

sell *(someone)* **down the river**

to betray (someone): *The workforce felt that their trade union had sold them down the river by accepting a lower wage rate from management.*

like clockwork

smoothly, without any problems: *Everything went like clockwork on the day of the wedding.*

Do it Yourself

1 If a young man **takes a shine** to a girl how does he feel about her?

2 Write down an idiom which is similar in meaning to **take the bull by the horns**.

3 Fill in an idiom to complete the sentence:

Ted is quite good at chess but he's _____ as the winner of the tournament.

4 If you **give someone the brush-off** do you welcome his/her company?

5 Write down an idiom which is opposite in meaning from **not to touch someone with a bargepole**.

6 If you **have a soft spot for** certain people do you dislike them?

7 Fill in an idiom to complete the sentence:

Jock is determined not to join the football team and I don't think you'll be able to _____.

8 If you **take the plunge** do you go on hesitating without taking any action?

9 Fill in an idiom to complete the sentence:

The workers agreed to strike but some of them changed their minds and their colleagues thought that they had _____.

10 If arrangements go **like clockwork** do you find many problems?

13 Shop-keeping

Idioms in Context

Diane was **dead to the world** when she heard the phone ringing. She was very annoyed as she had been to a party and had not got home until **the wee small hours**. When she answered the phone she discovered that it was her mother asking her to work in her aunt's gift shop for the day. 'Oh, mum!' cried Diane. 'Can't you do it? I' haven't had nearly enough sleep.' 'Sorry, I can't. I'm **tied up** here all morning,' said her mother, 'and your Aunt Liz is really **under the weather**. She can't afford to shut the shop, especially when Saturday's her busiest day.' Diane **had her heart in the right place** and said, 'OK, I'll get down to the shop as soon as I can,' she said. 'Thanks Diane,' said her mother, 'but you'd better **get your skates on**. Liz usually opens the shop at 9 o'clock.' In fact, Diane was feeling **below par** herself, mostly because she had drunk too much wine the night before, but she had some coffee and set off for the shop. The shop was indeed busy and she was soon **snowed under with** requests from customers. Diane was **rushed off her feet** all day, helping people to choose gifts, wrapping the gifts and taking the money for them. She was **on the go** all day and did not even take a lunch break. 'Thank goodness today's over!' she sighed as she locked up the shop.

Know the Meaning

dead to the world

very deeply asleep: *Gerry was dead to the world and did not hear his alarm clock ringing.*

the (wee) small hours

very early in the morning: *It was the wee hours before Isobel finished writing her essay. The ball did not finish until the small hours.*

be tied up

to be busy, to be occupied with something: *I can't spare the time to come to lunch — I'll be tied up with meetings all morning.*

under the weather

unwell: *Kate' s a bit under the weather — she thinks she's getting flu.*

have one's heart in the right place

to have a kind, generous nature, although this might not always be obvious: *Nora sometimes criticizes unemployed people but her heart's in the right place — she helps out at a hostel for homeless people.*

get your skates on *(informal)*

to hurry up: *We had better get our skates on if we are going to catch the 6.30 train.*

below par

not as healthy or well as usual: *Lucy has left work early feeling ill — she's been below par all morning.*

be rushed off one's feet

to be extremely busy with no time to rest: *The restaurant was crowded and all the waiters were rushed off their feet.*

be snowed under with *(someone/something)*

to be overwhelmed with (someone or something), to have a great deal of (people or things) to cope with: *The village has been snowed under with tourists all summer. The students are snowed under with essays this term.*

be on the go

to be active or busy: *My friend has two little boys and they're on the go all day — they're so exhausting!*

Do it Yourself

1 If you are **dead to the world** are you awake and alert?

2 Are **the small hours** in the morning or afternoon?

3 If your boss is **tied up** is he free to see visitors?

4 Write down an idiom which is opposite in meaning to **under the weather**.

5 Fill in an idiom to complete the sentence:

The new teacher seems very stern but she _____ — she was kind to little Susie when she lost her lunch money.

6 If you ask friends to **get their skates on** are you telling them to go as fast or as slowly as they can?

7 If you are feeling **below par** are you feeling exceptionally well?

8 Fill in an idiom to complete the sentence:

The shops were full of customers on Christmas Eve and the shop assistants were _____.

9 If a firm were **snowed under with** orders would it be experiencing a quiet period?

10 If you are **on the go** all day are you lazy and idle?

14 Work Experience

Idioms in Context

The final-year pupils of St Mark's School were off to do work experience at local firms. 'This is not a holiday!' said the head teacher. 'The employers have been asked to **keep your noses to the grindstone**. They'll let me know if any of you are not **pulling your weight**. This is an ideal opportunity to try out some jobs before you decide on a career.' 'I can't believe they're making us work **for nothing**,' grumbled Jack. 'I thought they would **pay** us **peanuts**, but they're not even doing that.' 'Don't **look a gift horse in the mouth**, Jack,' said the teacher. It's generous of people to let you into their workplaces.' 'I pity the employer who gets Jack,' whispered Rena. 'He'll **not do a stroke** all the time he's there.' 'Can you believe he's going to work in the local bank?' asked Tim. 'He's very poor at maths. He'll **play havoc with** the customers' accounts.' 'That's because his father's a banker and he was able to **pull strings**,' replied Sheila, 'but it's not so bad as Meg working in the hotel restaurant. She can't even boil an egg. I'm telling my parents to **give** the place **a wide berth** while she's there!' 'What are you doing, Sheila?' asked Len. 'I'm helping the local doctor's receptionist. It's a very busy practice and so it's not going to be **a bed of roses**.' None of the pupils seemed particularly enthusiastic about the idea of work experience.

Know the Meaning

keep one's/someone's nose to the grindstone

to work very hard without stopping or make (someone) work very hard without stopping: *I'll have to keep my nose to the grindstone if I'm going to finish painting this room this evening. The new teacher believes in keeping her pupils' noses to the grindstone and always gives them lots of homework.*

pull one's weight

to do one's share of a task: *We have to get all these books packed up by tonight and so we'll all have to pull our weight.*

for nothing

without payment: *We did all that gardening for nothing — the old man didn't give us a penny.*

pay (someone) peanuts

to pay (someone) very little money: *Adam has a job washing dishes in a restaurant and he's being paid peanuts.*

look a gift horse in the mouth

to complain about something that one has been given: *You shouldn't complain about the job which your uncle found for you in his factory — jobs are scarce and you shouldn't look a gift horse in the mouth.*

not to do a stroke

to do no work whatsoever: *Dad's paying my brother to look after the garden but so far he hasn't done a stroke.*

play havoc with (something)

to cause a great deal of damage to (something), to ruin (something): *Heavy rain played havoc with the tennis championships this year.*

pull strings

to use personal influence or power to gain some kind of advantage: *Dick's father might have pulled a few strings to get him a job in the law firm — he's a judge.*

give (someone/something) a wide berth

to avoid having contact with (someone or something): *The Wilsons advised their son to give the boy next door a wide berth — the police had arrested him on a drugs charge.*

a bed of roses *(usually found in negative constructions)*

a very easy and pleasant situation: *I know Sally had a tragic childhood, but mine wasn't exactly a bed of roses.*

Do it Yourself

1 Write the missing word to complete the idiom:

*It is Bert's final year and he is having to **keep his _____ to the grindstone**.*

2 Write down an idiom which is similar in meaning to **pull one's weight**.

3 Do you earn a lot of money if you are **paid peanuts**?

4 Write the missing word to complete the idiom:

*The sweater which your aunt gave you is not fashionable but you should not **look a gift _____ in the _____**.*

5 If you keep doing jobs **for nothing** are you likely to become wealthy?

6 Is someone who does **not do a stroke** likely to be very busy?

7 If something **plays havoc with** your health does it have a good or bad effect on it?

8 Fill in an idiom to complete the sentence:

Matt's father is president of the cricket club and, if you want to become a member, he could _____.

9 If you enjoy a man's company would you **give** him **a wide berth**?

10 If a job is not **a bed of roses** are you likely to find it easy and pleasant?

15 A Drive in the Country

Idioms in Context

It was a beautiful Sunday morning and Kate and some of her college friends had decided to go for a drive in the country. 'Let's **blow the cobwebs away** before we have to start studying again next week,' Kate said. 'Good idea!' Paul replied. I've been **itching to** get out of the city all summer.' Jim and Tina were going with them but George had **turned his nose up** at the suggestion, preferring to go to the cinema. When the others were studying the map and choosing somewhere to go, Paul commented, 'Don't **get carried away**! We won't be able to go very far if we want to get back to the city before dinner.' 'You should be **calling the shots**, Paul. It's your car and you're driving. You choose the destination,' said Tina. 'Let's just set off and **play it by ear**,' replied Paul. After they had been driving for some time Kate said that she would like to **stretch her legs**. They all got out of the car and set off to climb a nearby hill. 'I'm **running out of steam**,' said Kate when they were only halfway up. 'Let's have a rest!' In fact they were all **making heavy weather of** the climb and decided to go back. As they **picked their way** through the mud Jim said, 'I didn't realize that I was so unfit. I'm going to the college gym next week.' The others made promises to join him.

Know the Meaning

blow the cobwebs away

to stop oneself from feeling tired and sluggish, often by going out in the fresh air: *I'm going for a walk along the seafront to blow the cobwebs away.*

be itching to (do something)

to be very eager to (to do something): *I was itching to tell Steve the good news, but I had been told to keep it secret.*

turn one's nose up (at something)

to treat (something) with contempt, to indicate that (something) is not good enough for one: *Martin's wife turned her nose up when he suggested staying in a youth hostel — she is used to luxurious hotels.*

get carried away

to be so enthusiastic about something that one stops behaving sensibly or loses self-control: *Amy always gets carried away when she's planning a party and spends far too much money.*

call the shots

to be in control, to be in charge and make decisions: *It seems to be his deputy, and not the president, who's calling the shots now.*

play it by ear

to do something without making any fixed plans beforehand: *I haven't thought of what I'm going to say to the committee — I'm just going to play it by ear.*

stretch one's legs

to walk about after sitting for a while, to go for a walk: *We have to change planes at London and we'll have time to stretch our legs.*

run out of steam

no longer to have as much energy, enthusiasm, etc as one did: *Rona and Millie were very keen to start their own dressmaking business, but they seem to have run out of steam.*

make heavy weather of (something)

to find great difficulty in doing something that should be easy: *The teacher thought that the essay topic was very simple and could not understand why the students were making such heavy weather of it.*

pick one's way

to go carefully: *We had to pick our way through broken glass to get to our front door.*

Do it Yourself

1 Write the missing word to complete the idiom:

   *I'm going for a stroll along the beach to **blow the _____ away**.*

2 If you are **itching to** go swimming are you reluctant to go swimming?

3 If you like something very much would you say that you **turn your nose up** at it?

4 Do people who **get carried away** remain in control of their feelings?

5 Fill in an idiom to complete the sentence:

   Fay's father is paying for the trip and he is insisting on _____.

6 Fill in an idiom to complete the sentence:

   We don't have a fixed route for our holiday in England — we're just going to _____.

7 If you **stretch your legs** are you taking a rest?

8 If you **run out of steam** would you still be full of energy?

9 Write the missing word to complete the idiom:

   *It was such an easy job but the young gardener **made _____ weather of** it.*

10 If you **pick your way** are you walking without paying any attention?

16 A Reluctant Model

Idioms in Context

'Patsy's grandfather's taken up portrait painting as a retirement hobby and she's **roped** me **in** to sit for him,' said Mel wearily to her mother at breakfast. 'It wouldn't be so bad, but I**'ve other fish to fry** today. I'm supposed to be going shopping with Kay, babysitting for Ruth and going to the cinema this evening.' 'Couldn't you have refused?' asked Mel's mother. 'Patsy can be very persuasive and it seemed best to **take the line of least resistance** and say yes right away rather than listen to her **bending** my **ear** about why I should sit for her grandfather,' Mel replied. 'Couldn't any of her other friends do it?' inquired Mel's mother. 'Not likely! Most of her friends had the sense to **steer clear of** her when they heard about the portrait painting. I would have avoided her, too, but she **caught** me **on the hop** when I was waiting to see my tutor. I knew that I should **beat a hasty retreat**, but it just wasn't possible. My tutor had seen me,' said Mel. Two hours later Mel was back, the portrait-painter fortunately having **downed tools** early because of poor light. 'It was really terrible,' groaned Mel. 'My leg **went to sleep** and I was very uncomfortable. He asked me if I would sit for him again next week but I made an excuse not to go. **Wild horses wouldn't drag me** back there again. I don't care if he never finishes the portrait.'

Know the Meaning

rope *(someone)* **in** *(for something/to do something)*

to persuade (someone) to join in (doing something), often when he/she might be rather reluctant: *Joan is trying to rope people in to take part in a charity walk.*

have other fish to fry

to have something else to do: *Jim asked me to go clubbing, but I have other fish to fry — I'm going to the cinema with Colin.*

take the line of least resistance

to take the course of action which will cause the least effort, trouble, etc: *I'm opposed to Tina's political ideas, but I couldn't be bothered arguing with her — I took the line of least resistance and kept quiet.*

bend *(someone's)* **ear**

to talk a great deal about (something) to (someone), although he/she might not want to listen: *I try to avoid Jenny because she's always bending my ear about how successful her children are.*

steer clear of *(someone/something)*

to avoid contact with (someone or something): *We're all steering clear of Petra — she's looking for volunteers to deliver leaflets.*

catch *(someone)* **on the hop**

to meet or find (someone) when he/she is not prepared: *Our parents certainly caught us on the hop — they came back early from holiday and we hadn't cleaned the house.*

beat a hasty retreat

to go away very quickly: *Paul beat a hasty retreat before his father could ask him to wash the car.*

down tools

to stop working, sometimes suddenly: *We were working in the garden, but it was so hot that we decided to down tools and go for a drink.*

go to sleep

(of a limb) to feel numb: *My foot went to sleep during the long car journey.*

wild horses wouldn't get/drag *(one to do something)*

nothing could persuade (one to do something): *Rick's terrified of flying — wild horses wouldn't drag him on a plane.*

Do it Yourself

1 Fill in an idiom to complete the sentence:

I've _____ to sell tickets for the college dance but I really don't want to.

2 Write down an idiom which is opposite in meaning to **have other fish to fry**.

3 Write the missing word to complete the idiom:

I knew that Rita wouldn't take no for an answer and so I took the _____ of _____ resistance.

4 Fill in an idiom to complete the sentence:

I'm getting out of here — I don't want Rob _____ about football all evening.

5 If you **steer clear of** certain people do you wish to talk to them?

6 Write the missing word to complete the idiom:

I was going to clean the kitchen before my mother arrived, but she caught me on the _____ with dirty dishes in the sink.

7 Write down an idiom which is opposite in meaning to **beat a hasty retreat**.

8 If people **down tools** do they begin working?

9 Replace the underlined phrase with an idiom:

I had difficulty in standing up as my foot had gone numb.

10 Write the missing word to complete the idiom:

Wild _____ wouldn't get me to go up in a hot-air balloon.

17 A Party is Planned

Idioms in Context

Alice and her twin brother Jamie were extremely excited. Their eighteenth birthday was **just around the corner** and they were planning a joint celebration for it. They thought that a late-night party at home would **fit the bill**. Their elder brother, Brian, however, had just depressed them by **throwing cold water on** the idea. 'You're mad even to think about it! Mum and dad will never let you have it at home unless they're in the house all the time and that would really **put a damper on** the proceedings.' The thought of this **cast a shadow over** the twins' plans for the next few days. They had a feeling that Brian was right and that their parents would refuse. Finally they decided to **grasp the nettle** and ask their parents if they could have a party at home. 'Certainly not! The house would **look as though a bomb had hit** it next morning,' cried their mother. Their parents **put** their **heads together** to try to find a solution and went back to the twins. 'We know you want a party and we don't really want to **throw a spanner in the works**,' said their father, 'but we don't want the house ruined either. We've decided to **meet** you **halfway**. You can have the party at home but we'll put up a marquee in the garden.' 'What a great idea!' said the twins together and rushed off to get on with their party plans.

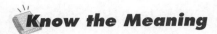

Know the Meaning

just around the corner

very near in time, soon: *I'm buying presents — Christmas is just around the corner.*

fit the bill

to be what is needed, to be suitable: *I've been looking for some dark blue curtain material and I think that this will fit the bill.*

throw/pour cold water on *(something)*

to be very discouraging about (something): *We had great fun making holiday plans and then Sid threw cold water on them by reminding us that we had no money!*

put a damper on *(someone/something)*

to lessen the enjoyment or enthusiasm of (someone or something): *We were having a wonderful time at the party when one of our friends took ill — and that put a damper on the evening.*

cast a shadow on *(someone/something)*

to make (someone or something) less happy: *The fact that the bride's grandmother was ill cast a shadow over the wedding.*

grasp the nettle

to tackle a problem or difficult task boldly: *Ned wasn't looking forward to telling his parents that he had failed his exams, but he decided to grasp the nettle that evening.*

look as though a bomb had hit *(something)*

to be in a very untidy state: *Dad's been looking for some papers in his study and the room looks as though a bomb had hit it.*

put heads together

to discuss something: *We're putting our heads together to see if we can find a way to get enough money to start a new club.*

throw a spanner in the works

to prevent something from happening, to spoil or ruin something: *We had the trip all planned and then Mick threw a spanner in the works by saying that he couldn't lend us his car after all.*

meet *(someone)* halfway

to reach a compromise with (someone): *Harriet wanted to work freelance at home, but the firm wanted someone to work full time in the office and so they decided to meet each other halfway — Harriet was to work part of the week at home and part of the week in the office.*

Do it Yourself

1 If an event is **just around the corner** is it likely to happen soon?

2 Fill in an idiom to complete the sentence:

Jean's looking for a green tablecloth — do you think this _____ ?

3 Fill in an idiom to complete the sentence:

The teacher should be encouraging the students but she seems to _____ all their ideas.

4 Write down an idiom which is similar in meaning to **cast a shadow over**.

5 Write the missing word to complete the idiom:

*The goalkeeper broke his leg and that **cast a _____ over** our team's victory.*

6 If you **grasp the nettle** do you avoid taking action?

7 What adjective would you use to describe a room that **looked as though a bomb had hit** it?

8 Fill in an idiom to complete the sentence:

Janet and Mark are going to _____ to try to find a solution to the noise problem.

9 Write the missing word to complete the idiom:

*We had planned to borrow my parents' caravan for our holiday but my dad **threw a _____ in the works** by saying that he had just sold it.*

10 If you **meet someone halfway** do you each insist on doing what you want?

18 Which University?

Idioms in Context

Mr and Mrs Shaw were discussing their daughter's university plans. 'I would rather that Donna went to the local university,' said Mrs Shaw. 'I think she might be **out of her depth** if she goes away from home. She's so shy.' 'Nonsense!' replied her husband. 'Donna's really **come out of her shell** during her last year at school. She's eighteen now and time that she **spread her wings**. I know you don't want to lose her but she can't stay **tied to your apron-strings** all her life.' 'That's not fair!' cried Mrs Shaw. 'I just want what's best for Donna. If she feels happy about going to university somewhere else, then I wouldn't **stand in** her **way**.' 'I'm sorry!' said Mr Shaw. 'I was only teasing and I know you'll miss her. All our other children have already **flown the coop**. Still I do think that living away from home would **do** her **the world of good** and increase her confidence. If she's in a student's hostel she'll be **rubbing shoulders with** all sorts of people.' 'I'm worried that she might feel **like a fish out of water**,' said Mrs Shaw sadly. Just then Donna came in saying, 'I've decided to go to university here because it's got the best course for what I want to do and I hope you don't mind but I've decided to share a flat with Cath and Netta. I think it's time that I begin to **stand on my own two feet**.'

Know the Meaning

out of one's depth

in a situation which one cannot cope with, often because of lack of knowledge, skill, etc: *Pete joined the college chess club but he was completely out of his depth — he is only a beginner and the others are all experienced players.*

come out of one's shell

to become less shy: *Sara was very shy when she went to school, but she soon came out of her shell when she got to know the other children.*

spread one's wings

to do things that are more ambitious or adventurous than one has been doing before: *Greg has been in the same job in the same town all his life, and he now wants to spread his wings and move to the city.*

tied to (someone's) **apron-strings**

too much under the influence or control of a woman, especially one's mother or wife: *Bill's mother seems to make all his decisions for him — he's really tied to her apron-strings.*

stand in (someone's/something's) **way**

to obstruct (someone or something): *If our daughter wants to go to drama school we won't stand in her way, although it is difficult to get work in the theatre.*

fly the coop (informal)

to leave home: *Now that all her children have flown the coop Madge has started on a university course.*

do (someone) **the world of good**

to have a very good effect on (someone), to be of great benefit to (someone): *Olive has been ill — a week's holiday in the sun will do her the world of good.*

rub shoulders with (someone)

to come into contact with (someone): *At the Youth Camp our students rubbed shoulders with students from all over the world.*

like a fish out of water

in a situation to which one is unaccustomed and which makes one feel uncomfortable: *Rose's friends are all keen on sport and she hates it — she's a real fish out of water when they all get together.*

stand on one's own two feet

to be independent: *June relies too much on her family — she should learn to stand on her own two feet.*

Do it Yourself

1 If you are **out of your depth** are you in a situation where you find it easy to cope?

2 Fill in an idiom to complete the sentence:

Her parents hope that Tracy will soon _____ — she's so shy that she won't talk to anyone.

3 Fill in an idiom to complete the sentence:

Frank wants to work overseas — he's tired of working on the family firm and wants to _____.

4 Write the missing word to complete the idiom:

*Charlie is 35 years old and still lives with his mother — he must be **tied to** her _____.*

5 If you **stand in the way of** a development do you encourage it?

6 If adult children **fly the coop** do they go on living at home with their parents?

7 Write the missing word to complete the idiom:

*Moving to a new house will **do** the family **the** _____ **of good**.*

8 Fill in an idiom to complete the sentence:

When students go to university they _____ people from many different backgrounds.

9 If a person is **like a fish out of water** does he/she feel comfortable?

10 If you **stand on your own two feet** do you rely too much on other people?

19 Attending an Auction

Idioms in Context

Ted and Bill were holidaying in a friend's country cottage. One day they went to the nearest village and saw an advertisement for an auction. Ted said that he would like to **have a go at** bidding for something and that they might get some real bargains. '**Pigs might fly**!' said Bill. 'Antiques are so popular these days and many people are **taken for a ride**.' Ted replied, 'that's more true of the big towns.' Bill said that **the well had run dry** to a great extent in the cities as far as antiques were concerned, and that more dealers were doing business in the smaller places. 'Besides,' remarked Bill. 'You have to be **on the ball** when you go to some of these small auctions. My father had an antique shop and he says that some of the articles for sale may well **have fallen off a lorry**. The auctioneers may be honest, but some of the dealers **sail close to the wind**. They reckon that in a small place people are less likely to realize that some of the objects for sale are fakes and so will not **blow the whistle on** them. Ted listened to all this, but he **never missed a trick** when there was a chance to make money and he insisted on going in to the auction room. His family were all interested in antiques and it would make them **sit up and take notice** if he came home with a bargain.

Know the Meaning

have a go at *(something)*

to make an attempt at (something), to try to do (something): *I'm going to have a go at cutting down this old tree.*

pigs might fly

an expression used to indicate that something is extremely unlikely to happen: *Mike says that he is saving up to buy a car — pigs might fly!*

take *(someone)* **for a ride**

to deceive or cheat (someone): *Madge was told that the second-hand washing machine was in working order, but she was taken for a ride.*

the well has run dry

there is nothing left in what was formerly a plentiful source of something: *The bookshop used to be a good place to buy antiquarian books, but it became popular with tourists, and now the well has run dry.*

on the ball

alert and sharp-witted: *It will be difficult to sell your old car to Sam for more than its worth — he's really on the ball with cars.*

fall off a lorry/fall off the back of a lorry

to have been obtained by dishonest or illegal means: *Jan's brother is selling cheap video recorders, but she's worried in case they fell off a lorry.*

sail close to the wind

to engage in activities which are not illegal but which come close to being so: *Some of the local traders sail close to the wind, although they have never been found guilty of selling stolen goods.*

blow the whistle on *(someone)*

to report (someone's) dishonest or illegal activities: *No one knew who broke the window until Charlie blew the whistle on Patrick.*

never miss a trick

never to miss an opportunity to gain some advantage or profit: *Jane has made a lot of money from her investments — she's never misses a trick.*

sit up and take notice

suddenly to start paying attention to what is going on: *We all thought that Mick was the least successful member of the family, but we sat up and took notice when he made enough money to buy a chain of shops.*

Do it Yourself

1 Write down an idiom which is similar in meaning to **have a go at** something.

2 If you use the expression **pigs might fly** are you referring to a situation that you think will take place?

3 If you take someone **for a ride** do you treat that person honestly and fairly?

4 If the **well has run dry** do you continue to receive a plentiful supply?

5 Fill in an idiom to complete the sentence:

If Frankie had been _____ he would have applied for a grant to fund his research project.

6 If goods have **fallen off a lorry** have they been acquired by honest means?

7 Write the missing word to complete the idiom:

*We were not surprised that Ralph ended up in prison — he always **sailed close to the** _____.*

8 If you **blow the whistle** on a friend do you keep quiet about his/her dishonest activities?

9 Write the missing word to complete the idiom:

*Trust Jim to find out about the free concert — he **never misses a** _____.*

10 If you **sit up and take notice** do you remain unaware of what is going on around you?

20 Election for President

Idioms in Context

The college election to choose a president of the students' Sports Club was only a few days away. Mark was hoping to be elected and most people thought that he **had a fighting chance**. His close friends were even more confident than that and thought that he would **walk it**. The only problem was that one of the new students, called Julie, had just decided to stand for the presidency and she was rather **a dark horse**. At first Mark and his friends weren't worried about her, because it seemed that she did **not have a ghost of a chance** of being elected. However, she was becoming very popular and was willing to **do a U-turn** on any of her policies, which were unpopular with the students, in order to gain more votes. Even some of Mark's supporters were thinking of **changing horses in mid-stream** and voting for her. It was time for his friends to begin to campaign more energetically and it was a case of **all hands to the pumps**. When the day of the election came Mark's supporters had worked hard and were fairly sure that he had the election **in the can**, but Mark was not so sure. He really wanted to win and was **on edge** all day waiting for the result. When this was announced, it was obvious that he had had no reason to be nervous. It was **a landslide victory** and Mark was the new president of the Sports Club.

Know the Meaning

have a fighting chance to

have a chance of success if great effort is made: *I want to go to university next year and my teachers think that I have a fighting chance if I study hard.*

walk it

to win or succeed easily: *I have an exam tomorrow but I've done so much work that I expect to walk it.*

a dark horse

a person about whose talents, abilities, etc little is known: *Jane has entered the talent show but she is rather a dark horse and we don't know how she's likely to perform.*

not have the ghost of a chance

not to have any chance of success: *David wants to go out with Jane but he doesn't have the ghost of a chance.*

do a U-turn

to change completely a decision, attitude, etc: *The union agreed to the pay rise at first but then did a U-turn and refused to accept management's offer.*

change horses in mid-stream

to change one's decisions, plans, etc in the middle of a project: *Frank has been studying History for a year but he wants to change horses in mid-stream and study Philosophy.*

all hands to the pumps

everyone must do what he/she can to help, especially in a crisis situation: *Granny is coming home from hospital tomorrow so it will be all hands to the pumps to help her settle in.*

in the can *(informal)*

certain, agreed: *Julie says that she does not know if she passed her exam but I think it is in the can.*

on edge

uneasy, apprehensive: *Joseph was on edge all day waiting for his exam results to arrive.*

a landslide victory

an election victory won by a very large number of votes: *The Prime Minister was delighted that he had proved his critics wrong and the general election had been a landslide victory for his party.*

Do it Yourself

1 If you **have a fighting chance** do you feel that you have no hope?

2 If someone says of a situation that they expect to **walk it** do they think that they are going to find it very difficult?

3 If someone is described as a **dark horse** do people know a great deal about him/her?

4 Write the missing word to complete the idiom:

*Lucy is hoping to run the marathon next year but she **does not have the ____ of a chance of finishing it.***

5 If you **do a U-turn** do you continue to take the same course of action?

6 Fill in an idiom to complete the sentence:

Tracey does not like her doctor, but she is not going to move to another one until after the baby is born, as she does not think that it is a good idea to _____.

7 If a situation requires **all hands to the pumps** would you expect other people to offer assistance?

8 If something is said to be **in the can** are you doubtful about the outcome?

9 Fill in the missing idiom to complete the sentence:

Vicky was ____ as she walked down the dark, lonely road.

10 If something is described as a **landslide victory** is it difficult to tell who has won?

21 Buying a Car

Idioms in Context

Mike was working in a factory during the college vacation because he had **set his sights on** buying a car. A friend of a friend knew someone that had one for sale supposedly at **a give-away price** and Mike went to see it. Mike knew very little about cars, and, when the man said that it **went like a dream**, Mike **took** his **word for it**. The seller took Mike out for a very short drive in it and Mike agreed to buy it. After he had handed over the money, he took it over to Joe's house. Joe, who knew a bit about cars, had a look at the engine and said, 'I don't want to be **a doubting Thomas**, but I don't like the look of this. My brother's a mechanic. Let's get him to have a look at it.' On the way to Joe's brother's house the car began to make a banging noise. When Joe's brother, Len, heard who the seller of the car was, he said, 'He's **a nasty piece of work**. Several people have accused him of **selling** them **a pup**.' 'Do you think that's what's happened to me?' asked Mike. 'I'm afraid **that's about the size of it**,' said Len, looking under the bonnet of the car. 'He really **pulled the wool over** your **eyes** when he sold you this and he certainly won't give you your money back.' Poor Mike! He had **learnt the hard way** not to trust everyone who is selling something.

Know the Meaning

set one's sights on *(something)*

to try to get (something): *I hope that the dress I have set my sights on is my size.*

a give-away price

a very cheap price, a bargain: *Let's go to the computer shop — I was told they had games at a give-away price.*

go like a dream

to perform or progress very well and smoothly: *Peter was delighted with his new motorbike because it went like a dream.*

take *(someone's)* **word for it**

to believe what someone says without question: *I have not read the book, but I will take your word for it that dad will like it.*

a doubting Thomas

a person who does not believe something: *Don't be a doubting Thomas — I'm sure that Matt will pay you back the money.*

a nasty piece of work

a very unpleasant person: *Dave warned me that the new manager is a nasty piece of work and he was right.*

sell *(someone)* **a pup**

to cheat (someone), to sell (someone) something that is useless: *I realized that I had been sold a pup when the computer would not turn on.*

that's about the size of it

that is an accurate assessment of a situation: *Donald thinks that he has failed his test and that seems to be about the size of it.*

pull the wool over *(someone's)* **eyes**

to deceive (someone): *He tried to pull the wool over my eyes, but I knew that he was lying.*

learn the hard way

to learn from one's own experiences (often unpleasant): *Susan learnt the hard way that she had to spend more time studying if she wanted to pass her exams.*

Do it Yourself

1 If you **set your sights on** something do you not care if you have it or not?

2 If something is for sale at **a give-away price** is it too expensive to buy?

3 Write the missing word to complete the idiom:

Steve said that the car usually **went like a** _____ *and he could not understand why it would not start.*

4 If you decide **to take someone's word for it** do you ask a lot of questions?

5 Is a **doubting Thomas** someone who has unquestioning belief in something?

6 If you are **a nasty piece of work** are you a nice person?

7 Fill in the missing idiom to complete the sentence:

Don't buy a bike from him — he _____ *last year.*

8 If someone says of your description of a situation '**that's about the size of it**' is he/she in agreement with you?

9 If you try to **pull the wool over (someone's) eyes** are you being honest?

10 Fill in the missing idiom to complete the sentence:

I tried to tell him not to speed but he had to _____ .

22 Nearly a Disaster

Idioms in Context

The members of the Mortlake football team were on their way to see their friend, Jim, and he was not **flavour of the month** with them. As the player who usually scored most goals in their matches, he was **the golden boy** of the team and he had just injured his ankle. Furthermore, he had not hurt it on the football field but while **playing the fool** at a nightclub. 'What are we going to do about the match with Farnham? It's only ten days away. They'll **wipe the floor with** us without Jim,' said Matt gloomily. 'If he's not fit in time we'll definitely **meet our Waterloo**,' Nick agreed. However, when they reached Jim's house he was surprisingly cheerful. '**Look on the bright side**!' he cried. 'At least it's only a sprain — my ankle's not broken. The physio will soon cure it.' Jim spent the next few days having treatment from his physiotherapist and soon declared that his ankle was **on the mend**. The other members of the team were very relieved when they heard that he had **got the green light** to play in the match. The Farnham team had been feeling very confident when they thought Jim would not be playing. However, when the match started they soon realized that they were unlikely to **carry the day**. The Mortlake team all played exceptionally well and scored **a hat-trick**. In the end Mortlake won 5-1 and Jim was carried shoulder-high in triumph from the pitch.

Know the Meaning

flavour of the month

a thing or person that is particularly liked by someone at the moment: *Computer games are flavour of the month with children at school.*

the golden boy/girl

a young man/woman who is talented and expected to do well in his/her career: *Tracey was the golden girl in her physics class.*

playing the fool

to act in a silly way, especially to amuse other people: *James did not do well at school because he was usually too busy playing the fool to listen to the teachers.*

wipe the floor with (someone)

to defeat (someone) completely: *Tom will wipe the floor with Bill in the golf tournament.*

meet (one's) **Waterloo**

to be finally defeated: *'It's time to meet our Waterloo,' said the captain of the team as they went out on the pitch to play the champions.*

look on the bright side

to be hopeful and look for the best in a situation, to be optimistic: *It may be raining but look on the bright side — the flowers are getting watered.*

on the mend

getting better: *June has been off work with the flu but she is on the mend now.*

get the green light

to receive permission to begin doing something: *Richard got the green light from his bank to go ahead with buying the house.*

carry the day

to gain victory: *'We may be missing our best player but we can still carry the day if we play as well as we can,' said the coach to his team.*

a hat-trick

an action done successfully three times in a row: *The crowd cheered with delight as William scored his hat-trick.*

Do it Yourself

1 If something is **flavour of the month** is it unpopular?

2 If someone is called the **golden boy** is he expected to do badly?

3 Fill in the missing idiom to complete the sentence:

David was embarrassed when his boss told him to stop _____ during meetings.

4 If you **wipe the floor with** someone have they beaten you?

5 Write the missing word to complete the idiom:

*'I have a feeling I'm about to **meet my** _____,' said Lesley as she walked on to the tennis court.*

6 If you **look on the bright side** do you believe that there is no hope?

7 If you are **on the mend** is your situation improving?

8 Write down an idiom which is opposite in meaning to **get the green light**.

9 If you **carry the day** have you been defeated?

10 If you score a **hat-trick** how many times have you scored?

23 An Unwelcome Friend Returns

Idioms in Context

Mrs Jacobs looked as though **something was preying on her mind** and indeed it was. She told her husband about her worries when he came in from work. 'Darren Murray's back in town,' she said miserably. 'What?' cried Mr Jacobs, 'I thought that he was still **behind bars**!' 'Apparently he's back living with his sister,' replied Mrs Jacobs. 'She says that he **has done his time** and wants to get a job and make a fresh start.' 'You can **take that with a pinch of salt**,' said Mr Jacobs. 'He may say that he's going to **keep his nose clean** from now on, but what about the old man he attacked?' 'His sister says that Darren didn't hit the security guard. It was one of the others, but they escaped and he was left to **carry the can**,' Mrs Jacobs informed her husband. When Darren had been sent to prison, the Jacobs had hoped that they had **seen the last of** him. Before he had got into trouble, he had been a close friend of their daughter, Chris, but they thought that she had **lost touch with** him when he went to prison. Now they were hoping that Darren and Chris would not **pick up where they had left off** now that he was back home. They were worrying unnecessarily. When Chris arrived home she said, 'You'll never guess who rang me today! Darren Murray. I told him to **get lost**.'

Know the Meaning

something is preying on one's mind

something is causing one constant unhappiness or distress: *Colin could not sleep at night because his forthcoming exams are preying on his mind.*

be behind bars

be in prison: *He should be behind bars for causing the accident.*

have done one's time

to have paid the price for committing a wrongful act: *Henry has done his time and we should forgive him and let him start a new life.*

take *(something)* **with a pinch of salt**

to have doubts about (something), to doubt that (something) is completely true: *Mary says that she is never going to be late again, but you can take that with a pinch of salt.*

keep your nose clean *(informal)*

to keep out of trouble by not behaving badly: *'If you don't want to end up in prison you had better keep your nose clean,' said the police officer to Fred.*

carry the can *(informal)*

to take the blame: *'It was your idea and so you can carry the can,' said Julie to her sister.*

see the last of *(someone/something)*

to see (someone or something) for the last time, not to see (someone or something) again: *Susan said, 'I'm glad to see the last of this place,' as she closed the door of the house which she had just sold.*

lose touch with *(someone)*

to stop communicating with (someone): *Rachel and Leo used to be very good friends, but they lost touch with each other when they left university.*

pick up where you had left off

to continue to do something after a period of not doing so, often to start communicating with someone after a period of not doing so: *I hardly ever see my friend in Canada, but, whenever we meet, we just pick up where we left off.*

get lost

a rude way of telling someone to go away: *'I've told you that I don't want to see you — so get lost!' said Phil.*

Do it Yourself

1 If something is **preying on your mind** are you able to forget about it?

2 Write down an idiom which is similar in meaning to **be behind bars**.

3 If a criminal has **done his time** is he still in prison?

4 Write the missing word to complete the idiom:

*John said that he will not steal again, but I think that I will **take that with a _____ of salt**.*

5 If you decide to **keep your nose clean** are you planning to get into trouble?

6 Write the missing word to complete the idiom:

*'I would like to help you but it was your mistake and you will have to _____ **the can** this time,' said Bob's mother.*

7 If you have **seen the last of** someone do you expect to see him/her again?

8 Write the missing word to complete the idiom:

*Jean hopes that she will not **lose _____ with** her brother when he moves to Australia.*

9 Fill in an idiom to complete the sentence:

Peter and Sharon used to go out with each other before they went away to university, and now that they have both come home they are hoping that they can _____.

10 If people tell you to **get lost** do they want you to stay with them?

24 An Anniversary Dinner

Idioms in Context

'It's mum and dad's twenty-fifth wedding anniversary next week,' said Moira. 'We should **put on our thinking caps** about what to give them.' ' They're supposed to be given something silver but that would **cost an arm and a leg**,' said her brother, Brian. 'Everyone will give them silver things. They'll get **stacks of** them,' said Moira's sister Lucy. 'I've **had a brainwave**!' cried Moira. 'Why don't we cook dinner for them?' 'I can't cook,' objected Brian. 'You can **do your bit** in other ways. You can do the shopping, for instance.' Finally they agreed that they would have a dinner party for their parents the following Saturday. 'We don't want to **bite off more than we can chew**,' said Lucy wisely as they were looking at cookery books. 'Let's do something simple. Dad **has a weakness for** this chicken dish with ginger and pineapple. It's easy to cook and it won't **break the bank**. We can have a salad to start with and fruit and cheese for dessert.' This sounded fine to the others. On the morning of the dinner party, Moira went into the kitchen and said, 'It's time to **clear the decks** and start on our preparations.' Brian went off to the supermarket with a list of what he was to get. 'He **has a memory like a sieve**,' said Lucy. 'I hope he remembers everything.' He did indeed get everything and their parents were absolutely delighted with their anniversary meal.

Know the Meaning

put on your thinking cap

to think of a way to solve a problem: *Emily realized that it was time to put on her thinking cap when she did not have enough money to pay her bills.*

cost an arm and a leg *(informal)*

to be very expensive: *The computer game was one that Robert had always wanted but it cost an arm and a leg.*

stacks of *(something) (informal)*

a large amount of (something): *'I don't need any more glasses — I've got stacks of them,' said David.*

have a brainwave

to have a sudden good idea: *Julie was trying to think of ways to make money and had a brainwave — she would offer her services as a babysitter.*

do one's bit

to do one's fair share of a task: *'We've both got full-time jobs now. It's important that you do your bit at home,' said Jean to her husband.*

bite off more than one can chew

to try to do more than one is able to: *'I would like to study medicine,' said Frances, 'but I don't want to bite off more than I can chew.'*

have a weakness for *(someone/something)*

to have a liking for someone or something: *Debbie is trying to lose weight, but is finding it difficult because she has a weakness for chocolate.*

break the bank

to leave someone without any money: *Maureen wanted to go on holiday to Jamaica but she realized that doing so would break the bank.*

clear the decks

to tidy up and remove unnecessary items in preparation for starting a task: *Before James began to make the Christmas dinner he decided to clear the decks.*

have a memory like a sieve

to be very forgetful: *Jenny asked Frank to get her prescription from the chemist, but he has a memory like a sieve and forgot about it.*

Do it Yourself

1 If you **put on your thinking cap** have you decided to ignore a problem?

2 If something **costs an arm and a leg** is it cheap or expensive?

3 If you have **stacks of** something do you not have enough?

4 If you **have a brainwave** have you thought of an answer to a problem?

5 Write down an idiom which is similar in meaning to **do one's bit**.

6 Fill in an idiom to complete the sentence:

Sylvia wanted to start her own business, but she did not want _____.

7 If you **have a weakness for** something do you like or dislike it?

8 If you **break the bank** are you left with a lot of money?

9 Write the missing word to complete the idiom:

*Joseph decided to _____ **the decks** before he began to fix the broken shelf.*

10 If you **have a memory like a sieve** are you good at remembering things?

25 A Marathon

Idioms in Context

Early one Saturday morning Molly knocked on her brother's bedroom door, calling out cheerfully, '**Rise and shine!**' Her brother, Tony, told her that he had no intentions of getting up so early, but Molly reminded him that it was the day of the local charity marathon race. 'Why did I enter?' groaned Tony. 'I'm just not **up to the mark** for it.' 'Nonsense!' said Molly. 'You came **within an ace of** winning last year. Besides, Brown's, the local furniture firm, has said that they will give our children's charity £2,000 if you win.' 'I'll **give it my best shot**,' promised Tony, 'but my job in the city doesn't leave me much time for going to the gym. I'm not very fit. I would really liked to have had more time to train. Still, I'll try to **give a good account of myself**, since it's for charity.' 'You're too modest!' said Molly. 'You never **blow your own trumpet**, but you're a really good runner and you've got stamina. We all think you should **have a stab at** breaking the course record. Brown's will give us another £1,000 if you do that.' 'Oh well! It's **in the lap of the gods** now. The race starts in half an hour.' Tony was quite near the back for the first part of the race, but **came into his own** in the last mile. He **won** the race **hands down** and broke the record. Naturally his sister and her charity were extremely pleased.

Know the Meaning

rise and shine

an instruction to someone to get out of bed — usually in the morning: *'Rise and shine — it's a beautiful day!' shouted Peter's mother.*

up to the mark

up to the normal standard: *The restaurant used to be very good, but the meal cooked by the new chef was not quite up to the mark.*

within an ace of *(something/doing something)*

very near to (something or doing something): *I was within an ace of getting an 'A' for my last essay.*

give it one's best shot

to try one's hardest: *You might not get the job but you've got an interview, and it's worth giving it your best shot.*

give a good account of oneself

to do well: *I hope to give a good account of myself in my next set of exams.*

blow one's own trumpet

to boast, to praise oneself greatly: *You may have won the race but there is no need to blow your own trumpet.*

have a stab at *(something)*

to try to do (something), to have an attempt at (something): *I've never been ice-skating before but I'll have a stab at it.*

in the lap of the gods

a situation that is left to chance, the outcome of which is hard to predict: *I've studied hard — the results of my exams are in the lap of the gods now.*

come into one's own

to have the chance to show one's best qualities, skills, etc: *When Shirley got a chance to sing in public she really came into her own, although she was usually very reserved.*

win hands down

to win very easily: *I don't like playing tennis with Jane — she always wins hands down.*

Do it Yourself

1 If someone tells you to **rise and shine** should you stay in bed?

2 If you are **up to the mark** at something are you bad at it?

3 Write the missing word to complete the idiom:

*James came _____ **an ace** of winning the gold medal.*

4 If you **give something your best shot** do you try to do well?

5 Write the missing word to complete the idiom:

*I'm looking forward to making my presentation to the class — it gives me a chance to **give a good _____ of myself**.*

6 If you **blow your own trumpet** are you being modest?

7 If you **have a stab at** something do you decide not to do it?

8 Write the missing word to complete the idiom:

*We are hoping to have a barbecue on Saturday but it depends on the weather and that is **in the _____ of the gods**.*

9 If you **come into your own** do you fail to show your talents?

10 If you **win hands down** do you come close to losing?

26 Amateur Decorators

Idioms in Context

'How would you like to help me decorate my gran's bedroom?' Paul asked Alf. 'That's rather **a tall order**!' replied Alf. 'I've never tried hanging wallpaper before and I'm **all fingers and thumbs** at that kind of thing.' 'I'm just going to paint the walls, not paper them,' said Paul. 'There's **nothing to it**,' 'I've often watched my dad and brother do it.' 'Watching someone else do something is all very well,' said Alf wisely, 'but it will be **a different ballgame** when you try to do it yourself.' 'I know it'll be a bit like **the blind leading the blind** if we do the job together,' admitted Paul, 'but it might be quite fun and my parents are going to pay us. Decorators are **at a premium** so near Christmas and they want to surprise gran. If we **get our act together** we should get it done today.' Paul then went off to the paint shop with his mother to choose the paint while Alf **held the fort** and began to cover the bedroom furniture with dust sheets to prevent it from being damaged by paint. 'Gran's room's **like something out of the ark** with all that dark brown paint. Let's get something light and cheerful,' said Paul's mother. When they got the paint, Paul and Alf began work and **had broken the back of** the work by the evening. They finished it next morning and Paul's parents congratulated them on their good work.

Know the Meaning

a tall order
something that is very difficult to do: *Paul wanted to complete the return journey in one day, but he knew it was a tall order.*

all fingers and thumbs
awkward, clumsy at doing something with one's hands: *Jean tried her best to sew the hem of her skirt, but she was all fingers and thumbs.*

nothing to it
very easy: *'Come on, you can jump across the river — there is nothing to it!'*

a different ball game
an entirely different situation or matter: *I'm happy to lend you my bicycle, but lending you my car is a different ball game.*

the blind leading the blind
to describe a situation in which one person who does not know what he/she is doing tries to help another person who is in the same state: *James is a very bad driver — when he was trying to teach Margaret to drive it was definitely the blind leading the blind.*

at a premium
in great demand and therefore difficult to get: *The band playing at the concert was very popular and tickets were at a premium.*

get your act together
to get oneself organized: *Jenny usually left doing her homework until the last minute but this year she decided to get her act together and finish it ahead of time.*

hold the fort
to take temporary charge of a job, task, etc: *George was babysitting for his sister, but he asked Fred to hold the fort while he went to the supermarket.*

like something out of the ark
very old-fashioned: *My mother lent me a dress to wear to the party, but I can't possibly wear it — it's like something out of the ark.*

break the back of (something)
to complete the most difficult part of (a task): *I've got to hand my essay in tomorrow but at least I've broken the back of it.*

Do it Yourself

1 If something is a **tall order** is it easy to do?

2 Write the missing word to complete the idiom:

I would like to help you put up the shelves but I'm all ___ and thumbs today.

3 If someone asks you to do a task and says that there is **nothing to it** do you find it difficult to do?

4 Fill in an idiom to complete the sentence:

Studying for exams at school is one thing but when you get to university it's _____.

5 If a situation is described as being **like the blind leading the blind** do people believe that the people involved know what they are doing?

6 Give an idiom which is similar in meaning to **at a premium**.

7 Fill in an idiom to complete the sentence:

'I know that you are disappointed that you failed your exam but you need to _____ and start studying for the next one.'

8 Fill in an idiom to complete the sentence:

John was working in the newsagent but he asked if I could _____ while he went out for lunch.

9 If something is described as being **like something out of the ark** would you think that it is modern?

10 If you **have broken the back of** something have you still got all of it to do?

27 A Case of Mistaken Identity

Idioms in Context

Rachel was home from college for a few days with an injured ankle. She was not used to **having time on her hands** and all her friends were away. Because she was bored, she spent a lot of time looking out of the window and one afternoon she called out to her brother, Ian, 'There's someone who is **up to no good** at the house next door. He looked in all of the windows and now he's trying to open them. At first I thought he was **a peeping Tom** but now I think he's a burglar. I'm going to call the police and they can **catch** him **red-handed**.' 'That's a bit **over the top**,' said her brother. 'It's a bit soon to **press the panic button** if the man hasn't actually entered the house.' When Rachel **took the bit between her teeth**, there was usually nothing anyone could do to stop her and she went straight to the phone and called the police. 'The police will be here **before you can say Jack Robinson** and the man's still there. They'll soon **cook** his **goose**,' said Rachel with satisfaction. The police duly arrived and Rachel saw them talking to man in the garden next door, but they didn't arrest him. Instead they went round to Rachel's house and told her it was the next-door neighbour who had forgotten his keys. Rachel hadn't **known** him **from Adam** as the family had moved in while she was at college.

Know the Meaning

have time on one's hands

to have a great deal of free time: *Sheila has a lot of time on her hands now that her children have left home.*

be up to no good

to be doing something wrong or illegal: *I don't want to go out tonight and leave the children on their own — I think that they will be up to no good.*

a peeping Tom

a man who secretly watches people (often women getting undressed) through windows: *Jane reported the peeping Tom to the local police when she saw him at her bedroom window.*

catch (someone) red-handed

to find (someone)who is doing something wrong: *Greg had suspected that someone was taking money from the till, and then he caught Dave red-handed.*

over the top (informal)

too much, excessive: *I know you are angry, but I think that hitting the child is over the top.*

press the panic button

to react to an assumed difficult or dangerous situation by panicking and acting in an over-hasty manner: *Don't tell Dad that Heidi is late coming home from school — he'll only press the panic button.*

take the bit between one's teeth

to act on one's own without taking instructions from others: *Steve was tired of waiting for the phone-call from the actors' agency and so he decided to take the bit between his teeth and phone them.*

before you can say Jack Robinson

very quickly: *I expect that Joanne will agree to marry Ian before you can say Jack Robinson.*

cook (someone's) goose

to ruin (someone's) chances of success completely: *Being late for the audition really cooked Mike's goose — he now has no chance of getting a part in the play.*

not to know (someone) from Adam

not to recognize (someone), not know who someone is: *That man said hello to me but I don't know him from Adam.*

Do it Yourself

1 Write down an idiom which is opposite in meaning to **have time on one's hands**.

2 Fill in an idiom to complete the sentence:

I am suspicious about that boy who is waiting at the bus stop — I'm sure that he _____.

3 If a man respects other people's privacy is he likely to be called **a peeping Tom?**

4 If you **catch someone red-handed** do you know that he/she has done something wrong?

5 Write the missing word to complete the idiom:

Melanie slapped Pam for ruining her book and I think that her action was _____ the top.

6 If people **press the panic button** are they calm and in control of a situation?

7 If you **take the bit between your teeth** do you hesitate and decide to do nothing?

8 If something happens **before you can say Jack Robinson** does it take a long time?

9 Write the missing word to complete the idiom:

Oliver cooked his _____ when he was rude to his grandmother — she has not left him anything in her will.

10 If you say that you do **not know** someone **from Adam** do you regard that person as a close friend?

28 Deceiving the Boss

Idioms in Context

Jane was doing some photocopying when she saw Phil come tiptoeing through the office door. 'The manager will **flip his lid** when he sees you,' she whispered. 'You're an hour late again and you **look as though you had been dragged through a hedge backwards**!' 'Sh!' said Phil, 'I've been to an all-night party and I haven't been home to wash or change.' 'I wouldn't be surprised if the manager **gives you your marching orders** for this,' said Jane. 'You've been late twice already this week. You **don't have a leg to stand on**!' 'It's not the manager I'm worried about, 'replied Phil. 'He's **all mouth and trousers**. It's Mrs Ross, the deputy manager who's likely to sack me.' 'You'd better go and **face the music** and tell her you've arrived,' said Jane. 'Not likely!' said Phil. 'She'll sack me! If I **play my cards right** they'll think I've been here all morning. It would definitely be a mistake to go **cap in hand** and apologize for being late.' Despite Jane's objections, Phil decided to **chance his arm** and pretend to have arrived at the office on time. He explained his rough appearance by saying that he was feeling ill and indeed he was. He had a hangover, although he did not tell his employers why he was ill. His plan **worked like a charm**. The deputy manger was so sympathetic that she sent him home early in a taxi so that he could recover at home.

Know the Meaning

flip one's lid *(informal)*

to become very angry: *Don't tell Dad that I crashed the car or he will flip his lid.*

look as though one had been dragged through a hedge backwards

to look very untidy: *I thought that you were going to make an effort to look nice for the wedding, but you look as though you've been dragged through a hedge backwards.*

give *(someone)* **his/her marching orders**

to dismiss (someone) from a job, etc: *I had to give Jim his marching orders after I realized that he had stolen the money from the till.*

not to have a leg to stand on

to have no way of excusing or defending one's behaviour: *Debbie is hoping Steve will forgive her for going out with his friend, but she does not have a leg to stand on.*

be all mouth and trousers

to tend to talk a great deal but do very little: *The teacher threatened to expel me but he is all mouth and trousers.*

face the music

to confront the outcome of your actions: *Mrs Thomson is at the front door asking about her broken window — I suppose that it is time to face the music and admit responsibility.*

play one's cards right

to make the most of one's chances of success: *If I play my cards right at this interview I could get promoted.*

cap in hand

humbly: *Fraser went to his wife cap in hand and asked her to forgive him.*

chance one's arm

to take a risk: *It looks like it might rain but I think I will chance my arm and cycle to work.*

work like a charm

to be very effective: *Susan had a very itchy rash but the cream, which she got from the doctor, worked like a charm.*

Do it Yourself

1 If you **flip your lid** are you happy about a situation?

2 Give an idiom which is opposite in meaning to **look as though you have been dragged through a hedge backwards**.

3 Write the missing word to complete the idiom:

*The boss **gave Bob his _____ orders** after he was late for the third day in a row.*

4 If you do **not have a leg to stand on** do you have a good chance of winning an argument?

5 Write the missing word to complete the idiom:

*William said that he would fix my washing machine but he **is all _____ and _____**.*

6 If you **face the music** are you trying to avoid a situation?

7 Write the missing word to complete the idiom:

*If **you play your _____ right** Jill might agree to go out with you.*

8 If you go **cap in hand** to the boss and ask for more money do you act in a confident, bold way?

9 If you **chance your arm** are you certain about the outcome of a situation?

10 If something **works like a charm** is it of no use?

29 Unsuccessful Entertainers

Idioms in Context

'I've found a way of making some money for our holiday!' exclaimed Jeff to his friends Will and Nick. 'My sister's a teacher at the local school and she's asked us to entertain the kids at their end-of-term party.' 'Have you been **hiding your light under a bushel**?' asked Nick. 'I didn't know that you were a children's entertainer.' 'I'm not, but the person whom they booked has flu and I thought we could **try our hand at** it. Who knows? We might **strike it lucky**. If we're a success we might get other bookings and make lots of money.' Nick and Will were not very happy, but they reluctantly agreed. When they arrived at the school, Jeff's sister said that the party was **in full swing** in the school hall. Jeff said that he would go and **see how the land lay**. When he came back he said glumly, 'They're all **as high as a kite**. The head teacher is just **giving them a ticking-off**. I didn't realize that there would be so many of them. They're **packed** into the hall **like herring in a barrel**.' It was too late for the would-be entertainers to change their minds and they did their best to entertain the children, but in vain. The children were not impressed and shouted their disapproval. Jeff **lost his voice** trying to make himself heard. They were glad when it was over and Jeff said, 'I think we'll **draw a veil over** that. Entertaining children's not for us!'

Know the Meaning

hide one's light under a bushel

not to draw attention to one's talent or ability: *Richard is a very good painter but he tends to hide his light under a bushel.*

try one's hand at (something)

to see if one can do (something), to attempt to do (something): *I have never made a cake before, but I will try my hand at it.*

strike it lucky

to have good luck in a particular matter: *I do not know what to expect when I go on holiday but I hope to strike it lucky and find good beaches.*

in full swing

going ahead busily or vigorously: *The party was in full swing when I arrived.*

see how the land lies

to consider the conditions which exist before making a decision: *I think that I will look for a new job next year, but I will see how the land lies in my present job first.*

as high as a kite

very excited: *The children were high as a kite when they were told that they were going to the zoo.*

give (someone) **a ticking-off**

to scold (someone), usually mildly: *The manager gave Shona a ticking-off for leaving work early.*

packed like herring in a barrel

very tightly packed, crowded together closely: *The passengers on the bus were packed like herring in a barrel.*

lose one's voice

to be unable to speak because of having a sore throat, etc: *I could not join in the singing at the party because I lost my voice.*

draw a veil over (something)

not to discuss or mention (something) in the belief that it is better forgotten: *Philip used to be married but he tends to draw a veil over that.*

Do it Yourself

1 If you **hide your light under a bushel** are you publicly demonstrating your skills?

2 Write down an idiom which is similar in meaning to **try one's hand at**.

3 If you **strike it lucky** are you likely to be disappointed?

4 If something is **in full swing** is it just starting?

5 Write the missing word to complete the idiom:

*I want to ask my boss for a raise but I think I will **see how the _____ lies**.*

6 If a group of people are described as being **as high as a kite** are they depressed and quiet?

7 If you **give someone a ticking-off** are you pleased with that person?

8 If you and your friends are **packed like herring in a barrel** do you have lots of room to move about?

9 Fill in an idiom to complete the sentence:

Could you please make less noise? If I have to shout any more I will _____.

10 If people **draw a veil over something** are they happy to talk about it?

30 A Missing Boat

Idioms in Context

Giles was **walking on air**. He had a new girlfriend called Lisa and he was anxious to **make a go of** their relationship. Now he was planning a special day out. Knowing that she was **in her element** anywhere near water, he decided to hire a boat and row out to the nearby island where they could have a picnic, swim and explore the area. The only **fly in the ointment** might be the weather, but, in fact, it was a sunny calm day when the time came for the trip. They enjoyed themselves very much on the island, but when they returned to the boat mooring, their boat was not there. 'Now we're **up a gum tree**!' said Giles and Lisa began to **cry her eyes out**. 'How are we going to get back?' sobbed Lisa. 'My father will **foam at the mouth** if we're not back in time.' Giles couldn't think what had happened to the boat, which he had tied securely, and he had no idea how they were going to get back, but he tried to soothe Lisa. '**Accidents will happen**. Your father will understand.' Just then he heard laughter and two of his friends, Bill and Tom, appeared with the boat. 'We were just **having** you **on**,' laughed Bill. Giles was very angry but Tom just said, '**Keep your hair on**! You'll be back in plenty of time!' 'No thanks to you!' replied Giles angrily, as he grabbed the oars.

Know the Meaning

walk on air

to feel very happy: *Sheila has been walking on air since she got engaged last week.*

make a go of *(something)*

to make a success of (something): *Karen has really made a go of her restaurant — it's always full.*

in one's element

in a situation that one finds comfortable and pleasant: *Frank was in his element when they started talking about politics.*

a fly in the ointment

something that spoils a situation: *The only fly in the ointment is that I will have to miss the party in order to go to the concert.*

up a gum tree *(informal)*

in a hopeless situation: *If I can't find the key for the front door I'm really going to be up a gum tree.*

cry one's eyes out

to weep bitterly: *When I got the letter about failing my exams I cried my eyes out.*

foam at the mouth

to be very angry: *Dad was foaming at the mouth when I told him that I had forgotten to put petrol in the car.*

accidents will happen

things can go wrong unexpectedly for anyone: *Don't worry about the car — accidents will happen and at least you were not hurt.*

have *(someone)* **on**

to try to get (someone) to believe something that is not true, to tease (someone): *You're having me on — I don't believe Fiona's going out with Ben because they've absolutely nothing in common!*

keep one's hair on *(informal)*

to stay calm: *Keep your hair on — there's only a tiny scratch on your car's paintwork.*

Do it Yourself

1 Write down an idiom which is similar in meaning to **walk on air**.

2 Write the missing word to complete the idiom:

*John has been studying very hard for his exams. I think he is determined to _____ **a go of** it this time.*

3 If you are **in your element** are you likely to feel anxious?

4 Write the missing word to complete the idiom:

*I'm really happy to be moving to London but the only _____ **in the** _____ is that I will have to sell my house.*

5 If you are **up a gum tree** are you in a good position?

6 If you are **crying your eyes out** are you only slightly upset?

7 If you are **foaming at the mouth** are you calm and happy?

8 Fill in the missing idiom to complete the sentence:

I'm sorry that the eggs got broken when I dropped your bag but _____.

9 If you are **having someone on** are you telling the truth?

10 Write the missing word to complete the idiom:

*I'm only one hour later than I said I would be — **keep your** _____ **on!***

31 Opening a Sandwich Bar

Idioms in Context

Carol and her brother John had had what they thought was a brilliant idea, but they needed financial help from their father and he was far from keen. 'You're **putting the cart before the horse**,' he had said, when they had explained that they were going to open a sandwich bar on the pier. 'You should do your market research first and find out if a sandwich bar there is likely to be profitable. Don't **rush your fences**! In any case, you would **have your work cut out** to buy all the ingredients, make all the sandwiches and serve at the kiosk all day.' Two days later Carol came in looking so angry that her sister Freda asked, 'Who's **rattled** your **cage**?' 'Bob Wilson and his friend have **stolen a march on** us. They've opened a sandwich bar on the pier and I think they knew we were planning one. I bet Dad mentioned the idea to someone.' 'Stop treating Dad like **the villain of the piece**!' said Freda. 'In any case **money is no object** in the Wilson family. Bob's probably doing it for a hobby and he'll tire of it soon.' A few weeks later John and Carol had **changed their tune** about the sandwich bar idea. 'Apparently Bob's making so little money that he's decided that **the game's not worth the candle**. He's closing down the business right away and **chalking it up to experience**.' 'Thank goodness we took Dad's advice!' said Carol.

Know the Meaning

put the cart before the horse

to do or say things in the wrong order: *The couple have had a baby and now they're getting married — isn't that putting the cart before the horse?*

rush one's fences

to act in haste without care: *I should have found out more about the job before applying — I always tend to rush my fences.*

have one's work cut out

to face a difficult task: *Julie will have her work cut out when the baby is born.*

rattle (someone's) cage

to upset or annoy (someone): *You look furious — who rattled your cage?*

steal a march on (someone)

to gain an advantage over (someone), especially by doing something earlier than he/she can do: *Jim was going to ask Anne for a date, but Peter stole a march on him and asked her out first.*

the villain of the piece

the person responsible for doing something wrong: *It turned out that Tom was the villain of the piece because he had lost the map.*

money is no object

money is not important: *Money is no object as far as my health is concerned.*

change one's tune

to change one's mind, opinions or attitude: *You've changed your tune about the film since speaking to Paul.*

the game is not worth the candle

the project is not worth the effort, time, etc spent on it: *I did think it was a good idea to hold a charity jumble sale, but we made so little money that the game was not worth the candle.*

chalk it up to experience

to accept something unfortunate that has happened and to try to avoid the same thing happening again: *I'm annoyed that I failed my exam, but I suppose that I'll just need to chalk it up to experience and study harder next time.*

Do it Yourself

1 Fill in an idiom to complete the sentence:

Don't _____. I think you should get to know him better before you think about getting married.

2 Write down an idiom which is opposite in meaning to **rush your fences**.

3 If someone **rattles your cage** are you not bothered about what has been done or said?

4 If you **steal a march on someone** do you feel that you have been defeated?

5 If you are **the villain of the piece** are you innocent of doing wrong?

6 Write the missing word to complete the idiom:

*I felt like the **villain of the** _____ when Lynne pointed out that I had forgotten to pass on the message.*

7 If **money is no object** to you are you determined to keep costs low?

8 If you **change your tune** are you persisting with something?

9 If you tell someone that **the game is not worth the candle** in response to a description of a plan do you think that it is a good idea?

10 Insert the word which is missing from the idiom:

*I am upset that Jamie was unfaithful, but I may as well **chalk it up to** _____.*

32 Toothache

Idioms in Context

'I'm in agony!' cried Jack, 'I **didn't sleep a wink** last night!' Jack had toothache but was refusing to go to the dentist. 'Even thinking about the dentist's waiting room **gives** me **the willies**,' he said. 'It's because you always **get into a state** at the thought of a dentist that your tooth needs attention. You haven't been to a dentist for ages and you neglect your teeth,' said Jack's sister, Mo. 'What **a Job's comforter** you are!' said Jack. 'In any case, I'm just off to clean my teeth now.' 'That's a classic case of **locking the stable door after the horse has bolted**,' said Mo. 'Cleaning won't help your sore tooth now. I'm going to get Mum. She'll **crack the whip** and make you go to the dentist whether you like it or not.' Mo was absolutely right about this, but their mother asked her to take Jack to the dentist. Mo said, 'I'll go, but I can't make him go into the surgery. **You can take a horse to the water but you can't make it drink**!' Mo and Jack caught a bus to the dentist and Mo fully expected Jack to **turn tail** and go home. However, his tooth was so sore that he allowed himself to be led quietly into the dentist **like a lamb to the slaughter**. He not only let the dentist treat the tooth but also even made another appointment. '**Wonders will never cease!**' said their mother thankfully when she heard the news.

Know the Meaning

not to sleep a wink

to be unable to sleep: *I could not sleep a wink last night for worrying about my interview.*

give *(someone)* **the willies** *(informal)*

to make (someone) feel nervous and afraid: *That man that was staring at me really gave me the willies.*

get into a state

to become upset: *It's only a short essay that you have to do; there's no need to get into a state about it.*

a Job's comforter

a person who attempts to be reassuring but whose comments and suggestions often make things worse: *Dad tried to make me feel better about failing my driving test, but he was just a Job's comforter when he said that many people fail several times.*

lock the stable door after the horse has bolted

to take action which is too late: *The Wilsons fitted a burglar alarm after their house was broken into but it was really a case of locking the stable door after the horse had bolted.*

crack the whip

to behave in a very strict way: *The teacher cracked the whip and told the class to behave or she would make them stay late.*

you can take a horse to the water but you can't make it drink

you can encourage someone to do something, but you cannot force someone to do something which he/she does not want to do: *I showed Tara the library but she refused to take out any books — you can take a horse to the water, but you can't make it drink.*

turn tail

to run away: *I wanted to turn tail when it was my turn to be interviewed.*

like a lamb to the slaughter

meeting danger or difficulty quietly and without resistance: *Tom went into the exam room like a lamb to the slaughter.*

wonders will never cease

used to describe a situation which is very unusual and surprising: *Sheila was early for work today — wonders will never cease!*

Do it Yourself

1 If you have **not slept a wink** are you likely to feel refreshed and wide-awake?

2 Write down an idiom which is similar in meaning to **give someone the willies**.

3 If you **get into a state** are you calm and relaxed?

4 Insert the word which is missing from the idiom:

Frank kept telling me that lots of people fail university exams — he's just a _____ comforter.

5 If you **lock the stable door after the horse has bolted** have you anticipated a problem and acted to avoid it?

6 If you **crack the whip** do you let people do as they please?

7 Insert the words which are missing from the idiom:

I told him that it was out of my control — you can take a _____ to _____ but you can't make it drink.

8 If you **turn tail** do you stay where you are?

9 If you go somewhere **like a lamb to the slaughter** do you struggle to avoid going?

10 If you say that **wonders will never cease** about a situation are you saying that it is exactly as you had expected?

33 A Protest Movement

Idioms in Context

Some of the residents of the small town of Woodtown were **up in arms**. They had just discovered that a developer had applied for planning permission to tear down a very old church and replace it with a block of flats. That news really **put** their **backs up**. There were not many historic buildings left in the town and many regarded the church as **the jewel in the crown** of the town's architecture. A public meeting was called and a group of protesters vowed to **fight tooth and nail** to prevent the church from being destroyed. 'You'll never win. You have no chance!' said some of the town pessimists. 'We might if we **stand our ground** and let them see how serious we are about it,' said Mr Shaw, who had been appointed leader of the protesters. 'We're **armed to the teeth** with information on why the building should be preserved. Our efforts might just **bear fruit**.' 'Nonsense!' replied the chief pessimist. 'I wouldn't be surprised if planning permission has already been given and you're **flogging a dead horse**.' 'I don't think so. There's always a great deal of **red tape** associated with planning permission. I think we've begun in time,' said Mr Shaw. He was right and, in fact, the protesters were victorious. The old church had a preservation order put on it and the developer could not touch it. As far as the protesters were concerned, the planning officer had **turned up trumps**.

Know the Meaning

be up in arms

to be angry and to make a protest about something: *Ian was up in arms when he realized that the time of the test had been changed and no one had told him.*

put (someone's) back up

to annoy (someone): *It really put my back up when Helen started boasting about how much money she earned.*

the jewel in the crown

the most valuable or important part of something: *We had a lovely holiday but the jewel in the crown was our visit to Rome.*

fight tooth and nail

to fight fiercely and with all one's strength: *I'll fight tooth and nail to stop them from sending granny home from hospital before she is better.*

stand one's ground

to refuse to give in: *I've decided that I'm not going to go to university and I'm going to stand my ground, whatever my parents say.*

armed to the teeth

fully armed with the weapons, tools, information, etc required: *I was babysitting last night so I went armed to the teeth with nappies, rattles and toys.*

bear fruit

to produce results: *I have a feeling that his plan may bear fruit after all.*

flog a dead horse

to waste time on a subject or action that is no longer likely to produce successful results: *Trying to get a financial contribution from Mark is flogging a dead horse — he's just been declared bankrupt.*

red tape

annoying and unnecessarily strict rules and regulations: *It would be much quicker if you could cut through the red tape and just give me my passport.*

turn up trumps

to behave well or to do the right thing, especially unexpectedly: *John has a reputation for being mean, but he turned up trumps when he lent us money for the deposit on our flat.*

Do it Yourself

1 If you **are up in arms** about something are you happy about it?

2 write down an idiom which is similar in meaning to **put someone's back up**.

3 If something is described as **the jewel in the crown** do people value it?

4 Insert the word which is missing from the idiom:

*James **fought _____ and nail** to stay in his house when his landlord tried to evict him.*

5 If you **stand your ground** do you decide to give in about something?

6 Insert the word which is missing from the idiom:

*The soldiers were **armed to the _____** and ready to take on the enemy.*

7 If something **bears fruit** is it likely to be a disappointment?

8 If you feel like you are **flogging a dead horse** do you feel that you are being successful and that it is worth continuing your efforts?

9 Insert the word which is missing from the idiom:

*There is a lot of **_____ tape** to sort out before you can get married.*

10 If someone **turns up trumps** are you disappointed?

34 Feuding Friends

Idioms in Context

'I'm getting really tired of Lena and Paula,' said Linda to Mark. 'They've been **at daggers drawn** for weeks now and it's got worse recently. They're not speaking to each other. In fact they're **giving** each other **the cold shoulder**.' 'I know,' replied Mark, 'It was bad enough when they were **spoiling for a fight** every time they saw each other, but ignoring each other is even worse.' 'There's obviously **a bone of contention** between them, but no-one knows what it is,' said Linda. 'It began at Julie's party last summer. From that night on Paula has only to come into a room to **make** Lena's **hackles rise** and Lena can **ruffle** Paula's **feathers** with just a look. They create such a bad atmosphere in a room for the rest of us.' Mark replied, 'I think that we should tell them that we are all tired of trying to **pour oil on troubled waters** on their relationship and that, if they don't agree to start talking to each other and stop quarrelling, then none of us is going to be friends with them ever again. Quite honestly, when we're in their company we spend all our time trying to **mend fences**.' 'I think you're right,' agreed Linda. 'We should **hold** a **pistol to** their **heads** tonight and tell them that if they're not prepared to **sink** their **differences**, then we don't want to know them.' 'Let's do that,' said Mark. 'I'll go and tell the rest of the gang.'

Know the Meaning

at daggers drawn

ready to start fighting or quarrelling at any minute: *Tricia and Brian have been at daggers drawn ever since their divorce.*

give *(someone)* **the cold shoulder**

to ignore (someone) deliberately: *I saw John in the supermarket but I just gave him the cold shoulder — he treated my friend very badly.*

be spoiling for a fight

to be eager to have a fight or quarrel, to be in an argumentative mood: *I'd stay away from Helen if I were you — she's in a foul mood and I think she's spoiling for a fight.*

a bone of contention

a cause of argument: *Paul and Michelle don't get on very well these days — that car crash is still a bone of contention between them.*

make *(someone's)* **hackles rise**

to make someone angry: *Every time I think about that man stealing my purse, it makes my hackles rise.*

ruffle *(someone's)* **feathers**

to upset or annoy (someone): *I don't know what is wrong with Kati, but something has certainly ruffled her feathers.*

pour oil on troubled waters

to try to calm and soothe a person or a situation: *I tried to pour oil on troubled waters by explaining how the accident happened.*

mend fences

to put things right after an argument or disagreement: *I suppose that I should go and see her and try to mend fences.*

hold a pistol to *(someone's)* **head**

to force (someone) to do as one wishes, often by making threats: *My parents think that I should study more, and they're holding a pistol to my head by threatening to reduce my allowance.*

sink *(our, your, their, etc)* **differences**

to forget about past disagreements and try to get on with each other: *If we are going to be living in the same flat, I think that we should sink our differences and try to be friends.*

Do it Yourself

1 If two people are said to be **at daggers drawn** do they get on well with each other?

2 If you **give someone the cold shoulder** do you greet that person warmly?

3 If you **are spoiling for a fight** are you in a good mood and wanting to be friendly to everyone?

4 Insert the word which is missing from the idiom:

The issue of getting married has always been a _____ of contention for Jane and Peter.

5 If something **makes your hackles rise** does it make you feel calm and relaxed?

6 Write down an idiom which is similar in meaning to **ruffle someone's feathers**.

7 Insert the words which are missing from the idiom:

*I used to fight with my brother all the time — my mum was always having to **pour _____ on troubled _____.***

8 If you decide to **mend fences** with someone do you intend to continue an argument?

9 Insert the word which is missing from the idiom:

*I'll get you to finish that essay even if I have to **hold a _____ to your head**.*

10 If you and another person decide to **sink** your **differences** do you agree to keep remembering a subject over which you quarrelled?

35 Job-hunting

Idioms in Context

Luke and a group of friends were looking at the job adverts in the local paper. They had just finished their first year at college and were trying to find ways of **earning an honest penny** so that they could go on holiday. 'Here's one for you, Bert. Gardening. You**'ve got green fingers**,' said Fred. 'No way!' said Bert. 'It won't be growing plants. It'll be **donkey work** like digging and mowing.' 'What about window-cleaning, Mike?' asked Tim. 'That's definitely **not** my **cup of tea**,' replied Mike. 'I'm scared of heights. The thought of climbing a ladder **makes my hair stand on end**.' 'What's a cleansing operative?' asked Barry. 'It's probably a fancy name for a street cleaner. I do wish employers would learn to **call a spade a spade**,' said Bert. 'Here's an ad for a dog-walker,' said Mike. 'I once did that,' said Fred, 'and I really **got my fingers burnt**. The pay was very low and the dog bit me on the leg.' 'What about bar work?' asked Pete. 'The ad's for someone with experience,' replied Frank. 'Anyway if I worked in a bar I'd spend all night **under the influence**.' 'That's true!' agreed Luke, 'I think quite a few new barmen start off by **hitting the bottle**.' 'All this talk of drink is making me thirsty and we still haven't found jobs. Let's go to the pub and **drown our sorrows**,' said Barry. 'Good idea!' said Luke and they all agreed.

Know the Meaning

earn an honest penny

to earn money in a honest way: *Teaching may be hard work but at least I earn an honest penny.*

have green fingers

to be good at gardening: *Tracey has got green fingers — her garden always looks beautiful.*

donkey work

the difficult and unrewarding part of a task: *Donald is so lazy and he always gets someone else to do the donkey work for him.*

not *(someone's)* **cup of tea**

not something that (someone) likes or prefers: *I won't come swimming with you because it's not really my cup of tea.*

make *(someone's)* **hair stand on end**

to terrify or horrify (someone): *That horror film we watched last night made my hair stand on end.*

call a spade a spade

to say exactly and plainly what one means: *James is very frank — he always calls a spade a spade.*

get one's fingers burnt

to suffer as a result of action which one has taken: *I don't lend anyone money because I've had my fingers burnt too many times before.*

under the influence

drunk: *I would not let him drive me home because he was under the influence.*

hit the bottle *(Informal)*

to begin to drink too much alcohol: *John and his friends decided that they were going to hit the bottle after their exams were finished.*

drown one's sorrows

to drink alcohol in order to forget one's problems: *It is no use drowning your sorrows — the problem will still be there in the morning.*

Do it Yourself

1 If you **earn an honest penny** have you deceived someone to get money?

2 If you **have green fingers** do plants that you look after usually die?

3 Is **donkey work** usually enjoyable and interesting?

4 Insert the word which is missing from the idiom:

*When I saw the black shape in the graveyard, it really **made my _____ stand on end**.*

5 If something is **not your cup of tea** is it something that you like very much?

6 Insert the word which is missing from the idiom:

*I'm not afraid to call **a spade a _____** and I say that he is a liar.*

7 If you **get your fingers burnt** after doing something are you happy and likely to do the same thing again?

8 Write down an idiom which is opposite in meaning to **under the influence**.

9 Insert the word which is missing from the idiom:

*I'm worried about George — since he lost his job he's really been **hitting the _____**.*

10 Insert the word which is missing from the idiom:

*I'm so depressed about failing my exams that I'm just going to go home and **_____ my sorrows**.*

36 No Longer a Student

Idioms in Context

Tricia had just graduated from university and was trying to decide on a career. She was being given lots of advice by family and friends. Some said things like, 'Take what you can get. There aren't many jobs **up for grabs** just now.' Others said, 'Apply for as many jobs as you can find. Don't **put all your eggs in one basket**.' Tricia decided to be independent and ignore most of the advice. She felt that it was now time to **paddle her own canoe**. Having discovered what jobs were available she decided to **hedge her bets** by applying for several of these and sent in her CV. Eventually she was given an interview by three of the companies and was pleased to be given the opportunity to **show her paces**. She had thought of answers to what she might be asked before going into the interview rooms, but she found that they all **went by the board** because she was so nervous. However, Tricia was lucky enough to **have the gift of the gab** and she did not find the questions difficult. She just hoped that she had **come up to scratch** in at least one of the interviews and would be offered a job. Who knows? She might even have a choice of jobs. In the end it was **Hobson's choice**, but Tricia was very pleased with the job she was offered. As she sent off her letter of acceptance she couldn't help feeling that she had **crossed the Rubicon**.

Know the Meaning

up for grabs (informal)

ready to be taken, bought, etc: *The house next door is up for grabs — do you think that you might be interested?*

put all one's eggs in one basket

to depend totally on the success of one particular plan: *I would not put all my eggs in one basket if I were you — you should interview several people for the job.*

paddle one's own canoe

to be in control of one's own affairs without assistance from anyone else: *I know you like to paddle your own canoe but you can still ask people for advice.*

hedge one's bets

to act to protect oneself against possible failure, loss, criticism, etc: *I think I'll hedge my bets and cook enough food for ten people — someone may bring a friend along.*

show one's paces

to show what one can do: *Helen is really looking forward to the talent show because she thinks it will be a good chance for her to show her paces.*

go by the board

to be abandoned or cast aside: *Mary was meant to be on a diet, but that went by the board when she saw the chocolate cake.*

have the gift of the gab

to have the ability to speak fluently and articulately: *Paul could talk his way out of anything — he's really got the gift of the gab.*

come up to scratch

to do as well as is required, to reach an acceptable standard: *Kevin is nervous about going to university — he's worried that he won't come up to scratch.*

Hobson's choice

the choice between taking what is on offer or getting nothing: *I said that I would be delighted to go to the dance with Michael but really it was Hobson's choice — everyone else already had a partner.*

cross the Rubicon

to do something which commits one to a particular course of action without allowing one to reverse one's decision: *Jane had crossed the Rubicon after she had said that she would buy the house.*

Do it Yourself

1 If something is **up for grabs** is it unavailable?

2 Insert the words which are missing from the idiom:

I think that you should apply to the other college too and not _____ all your _____ in one basket.

3 Write down an idioms which is similar in meaning to **paddle one's own canoe**.

4 Insert the word which is missing from the idiom:

Don't _____ your bets — just say which dress you prefer.

5 If you **show your paces** do you hide your talents?

6 Insert the word which is missing from the idiom:

The holiday went by the _____ when John lost his job.

7 If you **have the gift of the gab** do you find it difficult to talk to people?

8 If you **come up to scratch** do you feel like a failure?

9 If you have **Hobson's choice** do you have a great many options to choose from?

10 If you **cross the Rubicon** do you feel that you can change your mind?

37 Holiday Disagreement

Idioms in Context

Sam had books in front of him, but he was only **going through the motions** of studying. He had just been told by his parents that they had rented a cottage in the country for their annual holiday and he was not happy. 'It's bound to be in **the back of beyond**,' he muttered. 'I'm not going to go! I'll go somewhere with my friends. I'll just go and ask mum if that will be OK.' His mother had just told him how pleased she was that he had done so well in his exams and Sam decided to **strike while the iron was hot**. Sam discovered that she was not sympathetic and, although his mother always seemed a very charming, pleasant woman, it was a case of **the iron hand in the velvet glove**. 'Your father works very hard to **bring home the bacon** to keep all of us and he wants to go on holiday somewhere quiet. It's important to him that we all go and that includes you. At least you won't have to **pay your way**.' It was obvious to Sam that his mother would not **shift her ground**. He knew that he would not be allowed to go away on his own **in the teeth of** her opposition. Suddenly his mother appeared, offering **an olive branch**. 'Why don't you ask two of your friends to come, too?' When Sam asked Jim and Dave they **jumped at the chance** of a free holiday.

Know the Meaning

go through the motions *(of something/doing something)*

to pretend (to do something): *I was at work today but I could not concentrate — I was really just going through the motions.*

the back of beyond

a very remote or isolated place: *I didn't buy that house because it was in the back of beyond.*

strike while the iron is hot

to act while the situation is favourable: *My boss was really pleased with me today and so I decided to strike while the iron was hot and ask for a pay rise.*

the iron hand in the velvet glove

ruthlessness or firmness disguised by apparent softness: *Don't be fooled by that teacher — she may seem easygoing but I can assure you it is a case of the iron hand in the velvet glove.*

bring home the bacon

to do something successfully, especially to earn enough money to support one's family: *Debbie's father looks after the house and her mother brings home the bacon. My boss said that I would get a salary increase if I bring home the bacon on this deal.*

pay one's way

to pay for one's own expenses: *I like having a job and being able to pay my way.*

shift one's ground

to change one's opinions: *Ron and Ken are having a political argument, and Ken has begun to shift his ground a little.*

in the teeth of *(something)*

against or in the opposition to (something): *John decided to leave school in the teeth of his parents' disapproval.*

an olive branch

a sign of a desire for peace: *I decided to hold out an olive branch to James and ask him to go out for a drink.*

jump at the chance

to take advantage of an opportunity eagerly and without hesitation: *If Helen asked me to go on holiday with her I'd jump at the chance.*

Do it Yourself

1 If you **go through the motions of something** are you giving it your full effort and attention?

2 If you go somewhere that is **the back of beyond** are you in a very busy and crowded place?

3 Insert the word which is missing from the idiom:

*My driving lessons have been going really well recently. I think I'll **strike while the _____ is hot** and apply to do my test.*

4 Insert the words which are missing from the idiom:

*My boss seems to be very pleasant, but it is a case of **the _____ hand in the _____ glove**.*

5 If you **bring home the bacon** do you supply most of your family's needs?

6 If you **pay your way** do you use your own money to pay for things that you buy?

7 Write down an idiom which is similar in meaning to **shift one's ground**.

8 Insert the word which is missing from the idiom:

*Dave and Jane have decided to get married **in the _____ of** her parents' disapproval.*

9 If someone offers you **an olive branch** are you being given an opportunity to forget an argument?

10 Insert the word which is missing from the idiom:

*You are so lucky to be offered that job — if I were you I would **jump at the _____**.*

38 Looking for a Corpse

Idioms in Context

Jane was **dying to** be a journalist when she left college. She was always on the look-out for interesting stories and sometimes she found herself **in hot water** because of this enthusiasm. One day she was walking with her friend, Olive, along some sea cliffs near where they were holidaying when she saw something unusual down below on the shore. As usual she had with her **bag of tricks**, a satchel containing notebook, tape recorder and camera. 'Look!' she said to Olive. 'That could be a dead body down there on the beach.' Olive laughed, saying, 'That idea's **off the wall** even by your standards. I can't see very well, but it could be a large piece of driftwood.' 'You should **keep an open mind**,' replied Jane and started to climb down the cliff. She was nervous, for the cliff was steep and slippery, but she soon **got the hang of** it and reached the seashore with just a few scratches and bruises. 'It was **a wild-goose chase**,' she called up to Olive although it **went against the grain** for Jane to admit this. 'It's an old oil can.' She was terrified about climbing up again, but **kept her wits about her** and was soon at the top, having acquired some more scratches and bruises. After her adventure she was glad to be back at her parents' holiday house where her mother looked at her and said, 'You look as if you **have been in the wars**.'

Know the Meaning

be dying for *(something/to do something) (informal)*

to want (something) very much: *I ran all the way home and now I'm dying for a drink.*

in hot water

in trouble: *You'll be in hot water when Dad realizes that you took his car.*

a bag of tricks

all the equipment, etc needed to do something: *I hope the plumber brings his bag of tricks with him when he comes to look at the sink.*

off the wall *(informal)*

strange, weird: *I don't understand Chris — some of her comments are completely off the wall.*

keep an open mind

to be willing to listen to or accept new ideas: *I don't usually like that sort of thing, but I'll try to keep an open mind.*

get the hang of *(something)*

to begin to understand how to (do something): *I think I'm finally getting the hang of driving.*

a wild-goose chase

an attempt to do something that has no chance of success: *Paul spent a long time looking for the old castle, but it turned out to be a wild-goose chase — it was destroyed by fire years ago.*

go against the grain

in opposition to a natural inclination: *It goes against the grain for Sharon to say no to a cream cake.*

keep one's wits about one

to be careful and alert: *If you are going to walk home through the park remember to keep your wits about you.*

have been in the wars

to have suffered slight injury in the course of a rough activity: *Joseph came home from school last night with his coat all torn — he looked as if he had been in the wars.*

Do it Yourself

1 If you **are dying for something** to happen are you excited and expectant?

2 Give an idiom which is similar in meaning to **in hot water**.

3 Fill in an idiom to complete the sentence:

The doctor looked in her _____ _____ and brought out some cough medicine.

4 If something is said to be **off the wall** is it usual and ordinary?

5 If you **keep an open mind** do you choose to ignore what other people say and stick to your own opinion?

6 Fill in an idiom to complete the sentence:

If you keep practising skating you will soon _____ .

7 If someone sends you on **a wild-goose chase** are you likely to achieve what you set out to do?

8 Insert the word which is missing from the idiom:

*It may **go** _____ **the grain** but I think that you should apologize.*

9 Fill in an idiom to complete the sentence:

If you want to beat Fred at chess you will have to _____ .

10 If you look as though you **have been in the wars** are you completely without scratches or bruises?

39 Flat-hunting

Idioms in Context

Flo and Jenny were feeling miserable. They were looking for a flat to rent and had just looked at one that was particularly bad. 'There was hardly **room to swing a cat** in it,' said Jenny, 'and it was so expensive.' The girls were prepared to pay **over the odds** for the right place in the right area, but there were very few suitable flats available. Just then Meg, who was also sharing the flat, arrived with some information that **put new heart into** Flo and Jenny. One of her friends, Rosie, was moving from her flat and suggested that Meg and her friends might like to **give** it **the once-over**. 'If you want to see it, we'd better **get weaving**. Rosie's landlord said that we can have it if we decide right away.' All of the girls **were taken with** the flat and Jenny said, 'I'm sure we can soon **lick into shape** and have it looking like home.' 'It's amazing to think that this one just **dropped into** our **lap** after all those hours spent looking at ads,' said Flo. The girls were on their way to the landlord's office to get the rental agreement all **sewn up**. The only problem was that he wanted them to move in straight away and the lease on their present flat did not come to an end for another month. They knew that their current landlord would insist on **having his pound of flesh** and make them pay the full amount.

Know the Meaning

room to swing a cat (*usually in negative statements*)

a very small amount of space: *The holiday was great, apart from the fact that the hotel room was so small there was barely room to swing a cat.*

over the odds

more than necessary: *I'm really annoyed because I've just found out that I paid over the odds for my car.*

put new heart into (*someone/something*)

to give renewed hope and encouragement to (someone or something): *Passing her exams has put new heart into Rebecca and she has decided to stay on at university.*

give (*something*) **the once-over** (*informal*)

to examine something very quickly: *Robert asked his uncle to give the car the once-over before he bought it.*

get weaving (*informal*)

to start moving or working quickly: *You had better get weaving if you want to get that essay finished for tomorrow.*

be taken with (*someone/something*)

to think that someone or something is very pleasing or attractive: *Jane seems to be very taken with her boyfriend.*

lick (*someone/something*) **into shape**

to get (someone or something) into an orderly or efficient state: *I expect that the new boss will want to lick the staff into shape right away.*

drop into (*someone's*) **lap**

to be obtained without effort: *You can't expect a good job to just drop into your lap — you'll have to get out and look for one.*

sewn up

entirely settled or arranged: *Dave was really surprised that he did not get the job because he had thought that it was all sewn up.*

have one's pound of flesh

to get everything that one is entitled to, even if it causes difficulties or unhappiness for others: *My job pays well but my boss expects to get his pound of flesh from me.*

Do it Yourself

1 If you are in a place where you have no **room to swing a cat**, are you in a spacious room?

2 If you pay **over the odds** for something are you getting a bargain?

3 If something **puts new heart into you** do you feel more hopeful?

4 Fill in an idiom to complete the sentence:

I think that I will get my lawyer to _____ the contract _____ before I sign it.

5 Give an idiom which is similar in meaning to **get weaving**.

6 If you **are taken with something** do you like it?

7 Fill in an idiom to complete the sentence:

The garden is in a bit of a mess but I'll soon _____ .

8 If something **drops into your lap** do you get it easily?

9 If something is **sewn up** is the outcome uncertain?

10 Insert the word which is missing from the idiom:

*Angela intends to **get her pound of** _____ from Vincent when they get divorced.*

40 A Jumble Sale

Idioms in Context

'I wish I could help my Aunt Alice!' said Una. 'She's **the salt of the earth** and she's very worried about the charity which she runs.' 'What's wrong with it?' asked Dorothy. 'Apparently **its days are numbered** unless they get more money from somewhere,' replied Una. 'We could organize a jumble sale to raise some money,' suggested Polly. 'The money we would get would only be **a drop in the bucket**,' objected Rachel. 'I think it's a good idea. Every little helps and it would encourage my aunt, 'said Una. 'It will be hard work but it won't be too bad if we get a group together and we all **pitch in**.' Una enlisted the help of other friends and they worked **at full stretch**, collecting various articles for the sale. It seemed that there was no shortage of people with things to give away. Her aunt could not be with them on the day of the sale but she said that she would **be with** them **in spirit**. The jumble sale **got off to a flying start** with many people queuing up before it opened. 'Those must be people who **have a nose for** a bargain,' said Dorothy, 'and yet some of this stuff is junk.' **From the word go**, all the stalls were busy and all the helpers got very tired. However, it was all worth it. When they counted the takings they were pleased to discover that they had **made a packet**.

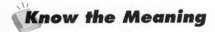

Know the Meaning

the salt of the earth
a very good and worthy person: *Rita spends all her spare time helping the homeless — she really is the salt of the earth.*

his/her/its etc days are numbered
the end of someone or something is imminent: *I think that I will have to get a new car soon because my old one's days are numbered.*

a drop in the bucket
a very small part of the amount that is needed: *Susan said that she could afford help in the shop one day a week, but that is really only a drop in the bucket.*

pitch in *(informal)*
to begin to do something or to participate in something, especially with enthusiasm: *The party will be a success if we all pitch in and make arrangements.*

at full stretch
exerting full power, energy, etc in doing something: *I would like to help you with your garden, but I am already at full stretch doing my household chores.*

be with *(someone)* in spirit
to be thinking of (someone), although not actually with him/her: *I can't come into the exam room with you, but I'll be with you in spirit.*

get off to a flying start
to have a very successful beginning: *The new girl at work has got off to a flying start by arranging a successful marketing deal.*

have a nose for *(something)*
to be good at discovering things: *Listen to Roger's plan — he always has a nose for a way to make money from nothing.*

from the word go
from the very start: *From the word go I knew that I was not going to get on with my new flat-mate.*

make a packet *(informal)*
to earn or make a great deal of money: *Jack's father made a packet when the horse won, but he lost it all on the next race.*

Do it Yourself

1 If a man is said to be **the salt of the earth** is he a selfish and unpleasant person?

2 Fill in an idiom to complete the sentence:

I think that I should start looking for another job — I have a feeling that _____ at the bookshop.

3 Give an idiom which is similar in meaning to **a drop in the bucket**.

4 If people say that they will **pitch in** are they being unhelpful?

5 Fill in an idiom to complete the sentence:

The bank manager refused to give Andy a loan because he thought that he was already _____ with his mortgage.

6 If you **are with someone in spirit** are you physically beside that person?

7 Fill in an idiom to complete the sentence:

The rowing team _____ but ran out of energy at the end of the race.

8 Fill in an idiom to complete the sentence:

I will ask the architect to look at the plans, since she _____ for design faults.

9 If you enjoy something from **the word go** does it take you a long time to discover that you like it?

10 If you **make a packet** have you been doing something which has proved to be unprofitable?

41 A Visit to the Gym

Idioms in Context

'I'm going to have to go on a diet,' said Jan. 'I'm going to be Lucy's bridesmaid in the summer and my dress is a bit tight.' 'You **eat like a bird**. You don't need to diet, but we would all benefit from some regular exercise,' replied Sonia. 'Why don't we join the local gym? Lorna's a member and she'll **show us the ropes**.' 'OK!' said Jan, 'and we'll ask Ros and Linda, too. **The more the merrier!**' When they arrived at the gym two days later they discovered Ros had bought a new designer outfit in bright blue Lycra. 'You know me! I never **do things by halves!**' she cried. The rest of them felt a bit ashamed of their old tee-shirts and track-suit trousers next to her, but they all chose an exercise machine and got to work pedalling, rowing or walking. At the end of half-an-hour Sonia said, 'I've had enough. I'm **sweating like a pig!**' 'And I'm **ready to drop!**' gasped Linda. 'Look at Lorna!' said Jan, 'we're all **dead on our feet** and she's **as fresh as a daisy**.' 'That's because she comes every week. She told us it was easy but I think she was just **lulling** us **into a false sense of security** to get us to go with her,' said Ros. 'I just hope all this exercise **works the oracle** and I can fit into my bridesmaid's dress,' said Jan. 'But all this exercise has made me hungry!'

Know the Meaning

eat like a bird

to eat very little: *I'm worried about Janice because she looks very thin and she eats like a bird.*

show (someone) the ropes

to explain or demonstrate (to someone) how to do something: *My boss is leaving me in charge when she goes on holiday, but she has promised to show me the ropes before she goes.*

the more the merrier

the more people there are the better: *I am only expecting a few people to come to the party but everyone is welcome — the more the merrier.*

to do things by halves (usually in negative statements)

to do things in a careless way: *My mother does not do things by halves and my sister's wedding was a lavish event.*

sweat like a pig

to sweat a great deal: *Brian was sweating like a pig after running for the bus.*

ready to drop (informal)

very tired, exhausted: *I've had a terrible day at work and I'm ready to drop.*

dead on one's feet (informal)

totally exhausted: *By the end of the party I was dead on my feet.*

as fresh as a daisy

very bright and lively: *I slept really well last night and woke up this morning feeling as fresh as a daisy.*

lull (someone) into a false sense of security

to lead someone to believe that everything is all right, safe, easy, etc when it is not: *Jim told Esther that her tournament opponent was not a good tennis player but he was lulling her into a false sense of security, because her opponent is last year's champion.*

work the oracle

to produce the desired result: *Rosie's studying worked the oracle and she did very well in her exams.*

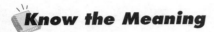

Do it Yourself

1 Give an idiom which is opposite in meaning to **eat like a bird**.

2 If you **show** people **the ropes** do you help them to understand how to do something?

3 Fill in an idiom to complete the sentence:

I've asked the whole class to come to the wedding, _____ .

4 Fill in an idiom to complete the sentence:

My father _____ — at the barbecue he made enough food to feed an army.

5 If you are **sweating like a pig** are you perspiring a great deal?

6 If you are **ready to drop** are you feeling very energetic?

7 If you are **dead on your feet** are you very tired and in need of a rest?

8 Insert the word which is missing from the idiom:

I feel as fresh as a _____ after that nap.

9 Fill in an idiom to complete the sentence:

I know that Harold said that everything would be all right but I can't help feeling that I've been _____ .

10 If something **works the oracle** is it a failure?

42 A Reluctant Shopper

Idioms in Context

'Where's Jock? Is he not coming to the match?' asked Will. 'No,' replied Tony. 'He's going shopping with Sara.' Will began to **laugh like a drain**. 'But Jock hates shopping and he loves football. He must be **off his trolley**.' Tony replied, 'He admits that he hates shopping, but he's **putting a good face on it** to impress Sara. He's **head over heels** in love with her. Earlier on he tried **playing for time** by helping his father mend his car, but Sara soon **ran** him **to earth**.' Meanwhile Jock and Sara were going round the shops in the high street. Sara loved shopping and was **having the time of her life** trying on a whole range of clothes. Jock was hating every minute of it. The high street was **crawling with** shoppers and the shops were all too hot for his liking. Worse, Sara kept asking him what he thought of the clothes which she was trying on. He thought that she was **as thin as a rake**, but she seemed to think that everything made her look fat. Jock kept saying everything looked fine, but, in the end, she didn't buy anything except a pair of tights. 'Isn't shopping fun?' cried Sara delightedly as they made their way home through the crowds. Jock was relieved to get home and went out to meet his friends for a drink later. 'A person would have to **have the patience of Job** to shop with Sara,' he groaned.

Know the Meaning

laugh like a drain

to laugh loudly: *I find it really embarrassing going out with Claire — she laughs like a drain and people always stare at her.*

off one's trolley *(informal)*

insane, very foolish: *You must be off your trolley if you think that I'm going to buy that car from you — it's a total wreck!*

put a good face on it

to pretend to be happy or satisfied when this is not the case: *Carol's putting a good face on it but she is really upset about breaking up with James.*

head over heels

completely, totally: *Pamela has fallen head over heels in love with Dave.*

play for time

to delay a decision or action to see if conditions improve: *I'm playing for time — I'm not accepting the job which I've been offered until I know if I'm getting a substantial pay rise at my present firm.*

run *(someone/something)* **to earth**

to find (someone/something) after a long search: *I finally ran Peter to earth in the gym after looking for him all evening.*

have the time of one's life

to enjoy oneself very much: *Thank you so much for asking me to come to the party — I had the time of my life.*

be crawling with

to be overrun with, to be full of: *The town is crawling with tourists now. Don't go into the kitchen because it's crawling with ants!*

as thin as a rake

very thin: *I don't think that Julie should go on a diet because she's as thin as a rake already.*

have the patience of Job

to be extremely patient: *You would have to have the patience of Job to teach in that school.*

Do it Yourself

1 If you **laugh like a drain** are people unlikely to know that you are amused?

2 If you make a suggestion and people tell you that you are **off your trolley** do they think that you are being reasonable and sensible?

3 Insert the word which is missing from the idiom:

   *Jack's **putting a _____ face on it** but I think that he is really unhappy in his new job.*

4 If you fall **head over heels** in love with someone are you not sure how you feel about the person?

5 If you **play for time** do you take immediate action?

6 Fill in an idiom to complete the sentence:

   I was trying to get in touch with Helen all week and I eventually _____ in the library.

7 If you **have the time of your life** are you likely to be happy?

8 Fill in an idiom to complete the sentence:

   I think that there must have been an accident since the High Street _____ police and I saw three ambulances.

9 If you are **as thin as a rake** are you overweight?

10 Give an idiom which is similar in meaning to **have the patience of Job**.

43 A New Session

Idioms in Context

It was the beginning of a new college session and the students were looking at the lecture schedule. 'Oh no!' cried Fay. 'I've got Mr Malcolm for English again. Apparently he used to be a brilliant lecturer, but by the end of last session he was really **losing his grip**.' 'I'm not surprised. He looks as though he has **one foot in the grave**,' replied Sheila. Just then Martin came up saying, 'I have to repeat the history course. I **made a hash of** the exam.' Fay was not sympathetic and remarked, 'You failed because you didn't do any work. **You've made your bed and you'll have to lie in it**.' Martin was hurt and replied, 'I could have worked **until I was blue in the face** and it wouldn't have made any difference. There were questions in the exam on subjects we'd never studied.' Next to appear were Julie and Jim. Neither of them was looking very well, as they had been **having a final fling** the night before returning to college. 'I hear Ms Baxter has left,' said Julie. 'She'll be **a hard act to follow**. I wonder who we'll get for Economics.' 'If it's Mrs Smith, I might as well **throw in my hand** now. I dented her car in first year and she'll no doubt **hold** it **against** me.' 'I doubt that and anyhow she knows the subject **from A to Z**,' Julie pointed out. 'I wish there were more lecturers like her.'

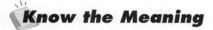

Know the Meaning

lose one's grip

to lose control or understanding of something: *The manger was under a great deal of stress and it was obvious he was losing his grip.*

have one foot in the grave

to be near death, especially because of old age, usually used as an exaggeration: *I don't think that Mr Jones should be in charge of the football team — he's got one foot in the grave.*

make a hash of *(something) (informal)*

to do (something) badly, to make a mess of (something): *I tried to make a delicious meal for everyone but I made a hash of it.*

to make one's bed and have to lie in it

to have to suffer the consequences of one's own actions: *Susan ran off with a married man and is now deeply unhappy, but her mother just said that she's made her bed and she'll have to lie in it.*

until one is blue in the face

having made maximum effort: *I shouted until I was blue in the face but the other climbers still could not hear me.*

have a final fling

to enjoy a last chance of extravagance or indulgence before one's circumstances change: *Sarah wants to have a girls' night out on Saturday so that she can have a final fling before she gets married next week.*

a hard act to follow

someone or something that sets such a high standard that others will have difficulty meeting it: *They've advertised my boss's job, but she's a hard act to follow.*

throw in one's hand

to abandon a plan, etc: *Julie had hoped to go to university, but she decided to throw in her hand when she failed her final school exams.*

to hold *(something)* against *(someone)*

to dislike (someone) or to think badly of (someone) because one knows that that person has done something wrong: *Although Ruth had joined a rival firm, her boss didn't hold it against her.*

from A to Z

very thoroughly and completely: *Anna was taught Italian cooking by her mother who knew the subject from A to Z.*

Do it Yourself

1 If you are **losing your grip** do you feel that you know exactly what you are doing in a particular situation?

2 If you **have one foot in the grave** are you very young and full of energy?

3 Give an idiom which is similar in meaning to **make a hash of something**.

4 Insert the words which are missing from the idiom:

*I don't have any sympathy for the boy who got sent to prison for stealing cars — **he's made his _____ and now he will have to _____ in it**.*

5 If you do something **until you are blue in the face** have you not tried very hard to do it?

6 Fill in an idiom to complete the sentence:

Steve is taking his wife on a cruise because he thinks she deserves _____ before going back to work full time.

7 Fill in an idiom to complete the sentence:

I feel sorry for the next captain of the team — Jim was very popular and he will be _____.

8 If you **throw in your hand** do you admit defeat and give up on something or do you go on trying?

9 If you **hold something against** your friend do you forgive him/her for something and act in a friendly way?

10 If you know something **from A to Z** do you have a very slight knowledge of the subject?

44 Out Goes the Boss

Idioms in Context

'Have you heard the news?' Jenny asked as she rushed into the office. Not giving her colleagues time to reply, she went on, 'Mr Moore has **got the bullet**!' Mr Moore was the head of the department and very unpopular. Everyone looked surprised. 'He's been here for years. I thought that he was **in with the bricks**,' said Ron. 'Apparently he's been **on the fiddle** for a long time and has embezzled thousands of dollars. The police have been brought in,' Jenny replied. 'I'm glad he's gone. He always **had a down on** me,' said Jock. '**I would like to have been a fly on the wall** when he was told to go.' Lucy said, 'You weren't the only one. I **fell foul of** him several times. He only liked people who were prepared to **lick** his **boots**.' John replied, 'That's true, but he's gone now and we can forget about him. **The burning question** is who will get his job?' Jenny said that she had heard that the deputy manager, Mr Brown, might be promoted but Bob, who had just arrived, said, 'He's **not a bad sort** but I've heard that they are going to advertise the job rather than promote someone in the firm.' Jean nodded in agreement, saying, 'I heard that, too. It's **a new departure** for this place. Still, it's a good idea to get someone new in.' Bob replied rather gloomily, 'Let's just wait and see who it is.'

Know the Meaning

get the bullet (*informal*)

to be dismissed from a job, etc: *Several people got the bullet when the two firms merged.*

be in with the bricks (*informal*)

to have been in a place, organization, etc for a long time and appear to be going to stay even longer: *I can't believe the physics teacher is going to another school because we all thought that she was in with the bricks.*

on the fiddle (*informal*)

making money dishonestly: *The manager had to sack the company accountant after she found out that he had been on the fiddle.*

have a down on (*someone*)

to be very hostile or opposed to someone: *I'm not surprised that I got a low mark for my history essay because the teacher has always had a down on me.*

(I etc) would like to be a fly on the wall

to be present at a situation without being seen so that it is possible to hear what is said without being involved: *I would like to be a fly on the wall when James finds out that Rachel crashed his car.*

fall foul of (*someone/something*)

to get into a situation where someone/something is angry with one or hostile to one, to get into trouble with (someone/something): *Jane fell foul of her boss when he found out that she had been late for work every day last week. Jack fell foul of the new speed restrictions and was charged by the police.*

lick (*someone's*) **boots**

to flatter (someone) and do everything which he/she wants: *Peter got promoted because he was always licking the manager's boots.*

the burning question

a question that is of great interest to many people: *Of course the burning question is who will win the election?*

not a bad sort (*informal*)

quite a pleasant person: *The new head teacher seems not a bad sort.*

a new departure

a change, something completely different: *It's a new departure for the café to sell evening meals, but it seems to be doing well.*

Do it Yourself

1 If your boss at work tells you that you have **got the bullet** are you being promoted?

2 If someone is said to **be in with the bricks** in an organization has that person just newly joined?

3 Fill in an idiom to complete the sentence:

Tom had better be careful that the tax department does not find out about his undeclared earnings — he's been _____ for years.

4 Give an idiom which is similar in meaning to **have a down on someone**.

5 If you **would like to be a fly on the wall** would you like to find out what is happening without anyone knowing that you are present?

6 If you **fall foul of someone** does that person treat you in a friendly way?

7 If you **lick someone's boots** are you trying to please that person?

8 Insert the word which is missing from the idiom:

The ____ question is will Sarah say yes to Roger's proposal.

9 If someone is described as **not a bad sort** is that person unkind and unpopular?

10 If your boss announces that the firm is intending to try **a new departure** do you think that it will continue to conduct its business in the same way?

45 Dancing Lessons

Idioms in Context

Mick was looking miserable when he arrived at Alice's house. When she asked what was wrong he said that he feared that **the writing was on the wall** as far as his relationship with Fiona was concerned. She had been his girlfriend for six months and had asked him to go to her graduation ball with her. However, he had never **got round to** learning to dance and there was to be formal dancing at the ball. He couldn't refuse to go as that would definitely **seal the fate of** his romance with Fiona. 'I thought things like waltzes and quicksteps were **as dead as a dodo**,' he said to Alice, 'and I **have two left feet**.' 'I'll teach you the basics,' replied Alice. 'You helped me with my geography assignment and **one good turn deserves another**.' On being told that the ball was to take place in ten days time, Alice said, 'We'll only have time to **scratch the surface**.' Mick hated the lessons at first but, after **a few false starts**, he began to enjoy himself. By the night of the ball he was becoming quite expert. Alice had persuaded him to hire an evening suit, although it was expensive, on the grounds that there was no point in **spoiling the ship for a hap'orth o' tar**. At the ball Mick's friends **did a double take** as they saw him gliding by on the dance floor. He was very glad that Alice had given him lessons.

Know the Meaning

the writing is on the wall

a sign that a disaster or failure is about to happen: *Derek realized that the writing was on the wall and that he would have to close down the factory.*

get round to *(something/doing something)*

to do (something) after a period of delay: *When John finally got round to ask Joanna for a date, she was going out with someone else.*

seal the fate of *(someone/something)*

to ensure that something, usually unpleasant, happens (to someone or something) in the future: *Laura knew that being late for work one more time would seal the fate of her chances of promotion.*

as dead as a dodo

completely dead or no longer useful etc: *I thought that flared trousers were as dead as a dodo, but I see that they are back in fashion.*

have two left feet

to be clumsy, especially in dancing: *John refuses to dance because he says that he has two left feet.*

one good turn deserves another

if someone does one a favour one should do that person a favour in return: *There's no need to pay me for fixing your washing machine — you put up those shelves for me and one good turn deserves another.*

scratch the surface

to deal with only a very small part of a problem, subject, etc: *Jane lent me some money to pay my debts but the loan barely scratched the surface of my financial problems.*

a false start

a beginning of an unsuccessful activity: *Jenny got off to a false start with decorating her bedroom when she hung the first two strips upside down.*

spoil the ship for a hap'orth o' tar

to spoil something of value by trying to cut costs: *Brian insisted on ordering a bottle of expensive wine to have with the meal — he said that he did not want to spoil the ship for a hap'orth of tar.*

do a double take

to look at, or think about, someone or something a second time: *Paul did a double take when Susan walked in with her sister, as he did not know that she had a twin.*

Do it Yourself

1 If you feel that **the writing is on the wall** do you feel optimistic and sure that everything is going to go well?

2 If you **get round to doing something** do you fail to do it?

3 Fill in an idiom to complete the sentence:

The opening of the supermarket _____ of several small shops in the village.

4 If something is described as being **as dead as a dodo** is it something that is very much alive?

5 If someone tells you that you **have two left feet** when you are dancing is that person complimenting you on your ability to dance well?

6 Fill in an idiom to complete the sentence:

I'm going to help Sam decorate his flat because he fixed my car for me last week and _____.

7 If you **scratch the surface** of a problem do you deal with it completely?

8 If you have **a false start** when doing something do you succeed at it instantly and without any problems?

9 Insert the word which is missing from the idiom:

*Debbie bought her daughter a pair of new shoes to wear to the ball because her new dress looked so lovely that she felt that it would be a shame to **spoil the _____ for a hap'orth o' tar**.*

10 If you **do a double take** do you assess the situation right away?

46 To Retire or Not to Retire

Idioms in Context

Peter's parents were having a disagreement. His mother wanted his father to retire. 'It's time you started to **take it easy**,' she said. 'You're **not getting any younger** and you've worked hard all your life.' Peter's father was not convinced. 'Most of my friends **are pushing** 60 and they haven't retired. I'm only 55,' he replied. 'You never **have a minute to call your own**,' Peter's mother went on. 'You need to get out of **the fast lane** and have some leisure time. Let the young people do more. They should be the **movers and shakers** of the firm now.' In fact Peter's father owned the firm and still liked to **keep his finger on the pulse**. The company had just secured a few very profitable export orders and was **going great guns**. He still had lots of business ideas and was not ready to give up working. The idea of staying at home every day horrified him and he was anxious to **put the kibosh on** his wife's plans for him. However, he knew that he would have to be very diplomatic or he would upset her, and so he proposed a compromise. He suggested that he would retire by stages and would start by taking one day off a week to spend time with his wife. This suggestion of some leisure time was **music to her ears** and she went off quite happy. Peter looked at his father and said, 'You handled that well, dad!'

Know the Meaning

take it/things easy

not to work, etc hard or energetically: *Richard had been over-working and was told to take things easy for a while.*

be not getting any younger

to be getting older: *Margie doesn't realize that she's not getting any younger and tries to compete with athletes who are much younger and fitter than she is.*

be pushing *(a certain age) (informal)*

to be nearly a certain age: *David's granny is amazing — she's pushing 90 but she still works in her shop every day.*

not to have a minute to call one's own

to be very busy working and to have very little time for rest or leisure: *I'm sorry that I haven't phoned you but I've not had a moment to call my own since my boss resigned.*

the fast lane

a competitive and highly pressured way of life: *Frank decided that he had had enough of the fast lane and retired to a country cottage.*

movers and shakers

energetic and powerful people who make changes or get things done: *Dianne is excited about her business lunch with the movers and shakers from that big law firm.*

keep one's finger on the pulse

to keep oneself informed about current ideas, events, etc: *The manager at the clothes shop is really good; she keeps her finger on the pulse and always manages to get the latest fashions in store before other shops.*

go great guns

to be doing very well, to be very successful: *I had difficulty with this essay at first, but now it's going great guns.*

put the kibosh on *(something) (informal)*

to prevent something from being done or from being successful: *I had been planning on driving down to visit some friends in the country, but bad weather put the kibosh on my trip.*

be music to *(someone's)* ears

to please (someone) very much: *It was music to my ears when James told me that I had passed my exam.*

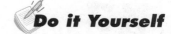

Do it Yourself

1 Give an idiom which is similar in meaning to **take things easy**.

2 Fill in an idiom to complete the sentence:

You shouldn't look after that huge garden by yourself — you're _____.

3 If you **are pushing** 30 are you just over 20 years old?

4 Fill in an idiom to complete the sentence:

Jane apologized for not coming to the party, saying that she has _____ since she had the baby.

5 If you work in **the fast lane**, do you have an easy and relaxed working life?

6 If someone describes you and your colleagues as **movers and shakers** does that person think that you are influential people in your work environment?

7 If you **keep your finger on the pulse** are you out of touch with the latest trends, etc?

8 If you are **going great guns** at something are you finding it very difficult?

9 If someone **puts the kibosh on** your plan does that person try to help you make it happen?

10 If something is **music to your ears** does it displease you?

47 Waiting for Results

Idioms in Context

Gemma was usually a cheerful person, but she had **had a long face** for days now. Her college exams had been more difficult than she had been expecting and she thought that she might well have **come a cropper** in them. All her friends kept thinking of things that might **take her mind off** the exam results which were not due for several weeks, but she could not help worrying. Tessa, in particular, was **making it her business** to try to cheer up Gemma. She had said to her, 'You **have a face like a fiddle** all the time and all your family are anxious about you. You should **keep your chin up** and hope that you've done better in your exams than you think.' Tessa had even suggested to Gemma that she join her in a holiday in the country. 'My Aunt Pat has a farm and there's lots to do in the nearby village. It would do you good to have a change of scene and Aunt Pat has said that it **makes no odds** if I bring some friends with me. She has plenty of spare bedrooms,' she had said. Gemma had spent a long time **humming and hawing** about the invitation. She didn't really want to **sweat it out** at home, but she didn't want to spoil Tessa's holiday. However, she had decided to go and was on her way, **bag and baggage**, to Tessa's house now.

Know the Meaning

have a long face

to look sad or disapproving: *Sam had a long face when I told him that I had changed my mind about going to the party with him.*

come a cropper *(informal)*

to suffer misfortune: *Billy came a cropper when he was driving his brother's motorbike.*

take (someone's/one's) mind off *(something)*

to turn (someone's/one's) attention away from (something): *I'm going to go to the cinema tonight because I've got my driving test tomorrow and I want to take my mind off it.*

make it one's business *(to do something)*

to be interested or determined enough to ensure that one does something: *Mrs Parkinson has really made it her business to find out who smashed the shop window.*

have a face like a fiddle

to look unhappy: *Fred had a face like a fiddle when he read his exam results — he must have done badly.*

keep one's chin up

not to get discouraged or lose hope in a difficult situation: *The doctor said that it is quite a serious illness but that I should keep my chin up.*

make no odds

to be of no importance: *It makes no odds to me if Sheila leaves town — I hardly ever see her now, anyway.*

hum and haw

to express uncertainty and be unable to come to a decision: *Dave eventually had to offer the job to someone else because Julie kept humming and hawing and would not make a decision.*

sweat it out *(informal)*

to endure a difficult situation: *My manager at work is really difficult to get on with but I've decided to sweat it out and hope that I can find a new job next year.*

bag and baggage

with all one's belongings: *Fiona moved out of the flat, bag and baggage, without saying goodbye.*

Do it Yourself

1 If you **have a long face** do you look cheerful?

2 If you **come a cropper** are you pleased with your good luck?

3 If you want to **take your mind off** something do you not want to think about it?

4 Fill in an idiom to complete the sentence:

   John should get charged for assaulting Bob and I'm going to _____ to see that he does.

5 If you **have a face like a fiddle** are you smiling and looking joyful?

6 Fill in an idiom to complete the sentence:

   The football coach told the team to _____ and try to play well in the second half.

7 If something **makes no odds** to you is it very significant?

8 If you **hum and haw** about making a decision do you find it difficult to make up your mind?

9 Fill in an idiom to complete the sentence:

   Helen is finding the work at university really difficult but she has decided to _____ until the end of her first year at least.

10 If you go somewhere **bag and baggage** do you go empty-handed?

48 An Allergic Reaction

Idioms in Context

Bill had been trying to persuade Danny to go riding with him, but Danny said that he **had something on** that afternoon. He had also asked Mark, but he said that he had not ridden for a long time and so was **out of practice**. Mark had suggested Leo because he had recently said that he would like to try horse-riding, and Leo appeared just as Mark spoke. '**My ears are burning**,' he said. 'What are you saying about me?' Bill explained the situation and Leo said that he would love to go horse-riding, but that he had never ridden before. 'Never mind,' said Bill. 'There are excellent teachers at the stables. You'll soon **feel at home** on a horse.' When they got to the stables, Bill went off to **do his stuff** and Leo was led over to what he thought was a very large horse. 'I **need my head examined** for coming here,' he thought in panic. As he mounted the horse, he began to sneeze badly and his eyes swelled up. '**What's up with** me?' he asked worriedly. The instructor said that Leo had had a very bad allergic reaction to horses and took him to hospital in his car. Leo felt **at death's door** but was all right after the doctor gave him an injection. The instructor said, 'You certainly **put the wind up** everyone. I think you'd better avoid horses in future.' '**You can say that again!**' Leo said with feeling.

Know the Meaning

have something on

to be busy, to have another engagement: *I would love to come to the party but I've got something on this Saturday.*

be out of practice

to not have had a lot of practice recently: *Jill asked me to go skating with her but I'm worried that I will fall because I am out of practice.*

one's ears are burning

someone elsewhere is talking about one, usually unkindly: *Rob's ears should have been burning last night — Meg and Jane were discussing how handsome he is.*

feel at home

to feel very relaxed, as if one is in one's own home: *I knew it was the perfect house for me to buy because I felt at home from the moment I walked in.*

do one's stuff *(informal)*

to perform in the expected way, to show one's abilities: *When the singer took to the stage and did her stuff, the crowd cheered.*

need one's head examined

to be foolish or crazy: *Denise needs her head examined for taking Andy back after the way he behaved.*

what's up with *(someone/something)*

what is wrong with someone or something: *What's up with Julie — I just saw her running down the road crying?*

at death's door

on the point of dying, often used as an exaggeration: *There was no way that I could have gone into work yesterday — I had flu and was at death's door.*

put the wind up *(someone)*

to cause (someone) to be concerned or anxious: *The manager really put the wind up Lesley when she told her that if she was late again, she would get the sack.*

you can say that again

you are absolutely right: *Jock came in and said that the weather was dreadful and we all replied, 'You can say that again!'*

Do it Yourself

1 If you **have something on** do you have nothing to do?

2 If you **are out of practice** at a sport have you played it recently?

3 If you feel that **your ears are burning** do you feel that people have been discussing you behind your back?

4 Fill in an idiom to complete the sentence:

It was a lovely holiday — the weather was great and we _____ in the hotel.

5 Fill in an idiom to complete the sentence:

Everyone was delighted when Sarah got up and started _____ on the dance-floor.

6 If someone thinks that you **need your head examined** does that person think that you are acting in a rational way?

7 If someone asks you **what's up?** does that person think that there is something not quite right?

8 Fill in an idiom to complete the sentence:

Alex says he feels _____, but he's only suffering from a hangover.

9 If someone **puts the wind up** you do you feel uneasy?

10 If someone says **you can say that again** to you after you have made a statement is that person agreeing with you?

49 A Missing Child

Idioms in Context

Jim phoned Bert just before lunch and asked him to go over to his house urgently. He said that he couldn't tell him what it was about, as the matter had to be **kept under wraps** for the moment. Bert was curious and hurried round. When he got there Jim's mother, who was **as white as a sheet**, told him that all the neighbours were **rallying round** to look for a little girl who had gone missing that morning. 'That man over there's a policeman and he's **running the show**, but he's **playing it cool** for the moment. He hopes that we'll find the little girl soon and he doesn't want the press **breathing down** his **neck** just now,' said Jim. Jim and Bert and the others set off to search the neighbourhood and Jim said, 'I hope she's OK. I **have a sinking feeling** that something awful might have happened. Somehow you don't expect these things to take place **on your own doorstep**.' The policeman called out to them to go and search in the wood behind the park, because someone had reported seeing a little girl there earlier. '**Reading between the lines** I think the police are more worried than they are pretending to be,' said Bert. Just then there was a shout from one of the searchers. The little girl had been found under a tree fast asleep. She was **none the worse for** her adventure, and everyone was extremely relieved to have found her.

Know the Meaning

keep (something) **under wraps**

to keep (something) secret: *Howard and Tracey are getting married, but they are keeping it under wraps until they have told their parents.*

as white as a sheet

very pale in the face, usually because of fear or illness: *Tom looked as white as a sheet when he found out that he had failed his exams.*

rally round

to come together for a joint effort or action, usually in a supportive way: *Ruth will be able to get out of hospital tomorrow if we all rally round and make sure that the house is ready for her.*

run the show

to be in control or charge of something: *I feel much happier about the holiday now that Suzie is running the show because she's a very good organizer.*

play it cool

to deal with a problem or situation in a calm way: *Paula really wanted the job but she managed to play it cool in the interview.*

be breathing down (someone's) **neck**

to come very close to (someone), often in order to watch him/her closely or to try to make him/her go or work faster: *My boss is never out of my office — he's breathing down my neck for the end of year report.*

have a sinking feeling

to have a feeling of pessimism or dread about a forthcoming event: *I have a sinking feeling that I am going to fail my exams.*

on one's own doorstep

very near to where one lives: *I expect that the burglar comes from another town — I don't think that someone would break into houses on their own doorstep.*

read between the lines

to understand more than is actually written or spoken: *Paul did not say why he was leaving but, reading between the lines, I think that he and Jane had a big argument.*

none the worse for (something)

to be completely unharmed by something: *Diane fell down the stairs but she was none the worse for her fall.*

Do it Yourself

1 If you try to **keep something under wraps** do you want everyone to know about it?

2 Fill in an idiom to complete the sentence:

Lisa was _____ after she crashed her car into the wall.

3 Fill in an idiom to complete the sentence:

The villagers had a meeting in the town hall and agreed that they would all _____ to raise funds to fix the church roof.

4 Give an idiom which is similar in meaning to **run the show**.

5 If you **play it cool** do you get over-excited?

6 Fill in an idiom to complete the sentence:

I find it very difficult to concentrate on driving when Roger is _____ _____ and telling me that I am going too slowly.

7 If you **have a sinking feeling** about something are you optimistic that it will go well?

8 If something happens **on your own doorstep** does it happen in a place very far away?

9 Fill in an idiom to complete the sentence:

I have not had my results back yet, but I was talking to my tutor yesterday and, _____, I think that I have got a really good mark for my essay.

10 If you are **none the worse for** something are you permanently injured because of it?

50 Up a Tree

Idioms in Context

'What's Pete doing with that ladder?' asked Matt. His friend, Joe, replied, 'Meg's family cat has got stuck up a tree and Pete's **got lumbered with** rescuing it. It's a big tree and the cat's far up it. He's going to **have a job**.' 'What's Meg's cat got to do with Pete?' asked Matt. Joe answered, 'Oh, he's **been all over** her recently. He'll be hoping to impress her by being **an angel of mercy**.' When they went to see how Pete was getting on, the rescue attempt seemed to be **hanging fire**. When asked why he hadn't gone up the ladder yet, Pete told his friends that he was trying to **put off the evil hour** as long as he could in the hope that the cat would come down without help. 'You should leave it to come down itself, anyhow,' said Matt. 'A cat is supposed to **lead a charmed life**. In fact, they say cats have nine lives.' Nevertheless, Pete climbed the ladder into the tree, but the cat ran further up. Just then the branch that Pete had climbed on began to break. He was **hanging on like grim death** and shouting for help. Someone phoned for the fire service and they must have been **quick off the mark**, because they were there in a remarkably short time. 'That was **a near thing**,' said Pete as he was led to safety. As for the cat, it came down the tree unaided.

Know the Meaning

get lumbered with *(someone/something)* *(informal)*

to be given an unwanted or unpleasant task or responsibility: *I got lumbered with paying for the meal for everyone because no one else had brought enough money.*

have a job *(informal)*

to have difficulty in doing something: *You'll have a job getting Peter to pay you back.*

be all over *(someone)*

to be over-friendly to someone, to make too big a fuss of someone: *Wendy was really embarrassed that Fred was all over her at the party.*

an angel of mercy

a person who appears, bringing help, when they are particularly needed: *Derek was an angel of mercy when he said that he could lend me the money for the deposit for the holiday.*

hang fire

to delay or to be delayed: *Our plans to build a conservatory are hanging fire until we have some more money.*

put off the evil hour

to postpone something unpleasant: *I suppose that I should open my exam results now — there's no point in putting off the evil hour any longer.*

lead a charmed life

to continuously escape from danger or harm with no ill effect: *Elaine leads such a charmed life — she's always late, but the boss never notices.*

hang on like grim death

to take a very firm hold of something in a difficult situation: *The instructor told me to hang on like grim death while she fetched a ladder.*

quick off the mark

acting in a prompt or speedy manner: *If Gillian wants to get that job she will have to be quick off the mark with her application.*

a near thing

the state or act of having narrowly avoided an accident or punishment: *Stan should drive more carefully — that was a near thing when he overtook that lorry.*

Do it Yourself

1 If you felt that you **have been lumbered with** doing something are you happy to do it?

2 If someone says that you will **have a job** doing something does that person expect that it will not be easy to do?

3 Fill in an idiom to complete the sentence:

Yvonne is so fickle, she _____ Bob at the party, but she totally ignored him when she saw him in the street the next day.

4 Give an idiom which is similar in meaning to **angel of mercy**.

5 If you decide to **hang fire** do you act instantly?

6 If you **put off the evil hour** do you decide to deal with a difficult situation immediately?

7 If you **lead a charmed life** do you always suffer badly?

8 Fill in an idiom to complete the sentence:

If you are getting a lift from Adam you will have to _____ because he always drives far too fast.

9 Fill in an idiom to complete the sentence:

Dawn was very _____ when I told her that there was a reward for the person who finished the work first.

10 If someone describes a situation as a **near thing** does that person believe that there was a strong possibility that there could have been some sort of misfortune?

51 Exam Nerves

Idioms in Context

The final exams were **looming large** and some of the students at Hampton College were looking distinctly worried. 'I'm never going to have time to study all the subjects,' groaned Jack. 'I think I'll **cut my losses** and concentrate on those subjects which I think I can pass.' Morag, who had done more studying than most of them, said smugly, 'It's a case of **chickens coming home to roost**,' she said. 'You should have done more work throughout the year.' 'Morag's right,' said Mike. 'If you'd kept up-to-date with the work, you would not be struggling now.' 'That's **the pot calling the kettle black**. You didn't do much studying throughout the year either,' answered Jack. 'I'm particularly worried about the maths course,' said Sheila. 'It's so difficult that several students left it because they couldn't **stay the pace**. The trouble is that my parents think I'm going to do brilliantly, which is just **pie in the sky**.' 'I'm going to be **in the soup** if I do badly,' said Jock. 'My parents keep telling me to work harder and I haven't. I'm certain I'm going to **make a pig's ear of** the economics exam. The lectures were all a bit **above my head** and the lecturer wasn't very good at explaining things.' 'I think most of us will need some luck if we're going to do well,' said Jean. 'Let's hope that we can all **pull a rabbit out of a hat** on the day of the exams.

Know the Meaning

loom large

to be about to happen and so to be very important: *I'll have to book more driving lessons because my test is looming large.*

cut one's losses

to decide not to waste more time, effort, etc on something one has already spent time, effort, etc on: *I'm taking golf lessons, but I don't enjoy the game and so I've decided to cut my losses and give it up.*

chickens come home to roost

a situation in which past errors committed by someone begin to have an adverse effect on him/her: *Mr Bruce would like to live with his children now that he is old, but he was a very uncaring father and all of them have refused — his chickens have come home to roost.*

the pot calling the kettle black

used to describe someone who is criticizing another person for doing something that he/she also does: *Pauline shouted at me for being late this morning but that's the pot calling the kettle black — she is never on time.*

stay the pace

to maintain progress at the same rate as others: *I've decided that I'm going to run the marathon next year since my coach thinks that I've got what it takes to stay the pace.*

pie in the sky

hope of success or achievement which has very little or no chance of being fulfilled: *Steve thinks that he is going to become a famous actor, but that is just pie in the sky.*

in the soup *(informal)*

in serious trouble: *Jane is really in the soup after crashing her car.*

make a pig's ear of *(something) (informal)*

to do (something) very badly: *Phil baked a cake for Caroline's birthday, but he made a pig's ear of it and had to buy one from the baker instead.*

above one's head

too difficult for one to understand: *Susan explained how to use the computer but I have to confess that it was all above my head.*

pull a rabbit out of a hat

to produce a very pleasant surprise: *Peter's business will have to close unless the bank manager can pull a rabbit out of a hat.*

Do it Yourself

1 If something is **looming large** is it imminent?

2 If you decide to **cut your losses** do you decide to persist with a project?

3 Fill in an idiom to complete the sentence:

Julie has left her husband after finding out he was having an affair, and I'm glad his _____.

4 Fill in an idiom to complete the sentence:

Helen said that I was a terrible cook but that's the _____, because everything that she makes tastes burnt.

5 If you **stay the pace** do you find that you are unable to keep up with others?

6 If someone says of your plan that it is **pie in the sky** does that person think that you have a realistic chance of success?

7 Give an idiom which is similar in meaning to **in the soup**.

8 If you **make a pig's ear of** something are you likely to feel proud of what you have done?

9 If something is **above your head** do you have no problem in understanding it?

10 Fill in an idiom to complete the sentence:

We had given up trying to get a package holiday to Europe that we could afford when the travel agent _____.

52 Misery at Work

Idioms in Context

Nora was not feeling very happy. Next week she was going on a training course in connection with her work and the manager of her department, Mr Scott, had said that the course would **separate the sheep from the goats**. Somehow Nora had **got off on the wrong foot** with him when she started work and things had not improved. Indeed, they had got worse and Nora thought that Mr Scott was **gunning for her**. When she was feeling exceptionally pessimistic, she wondered if he was just waiting for her to **fall flat on her face**. This was a pity because the job would be **plain sailing** without him. Some of her colleagues thought that it was **rough on** Nora to be in Mr Scott's department as the other managers were all much easier to work for. Several of them advised her to complain about his behaviour, but Nora would **run a mile** before she would draw attention to herself in such a way. She was very shy and lacked confidence, partly because she had always **played second fiddle to** her elder sister, Susan, who was brilliant. Also, Mr Scott was one of the most senior managers and she thought that she would be **wasting her breath** if she reported him. Nora attended the course and performed very well. Indeed, she did so well that she was promoted and was no longer in Mr Scott's department. She was now able to **thumb her nose at** him.

Know the Meaning

separate the sheep from the goats

to separate or distinguish the good from the bad or the worthless: *The teacher has said that she is going to give us a test next week and that she expects that it will separate the sheep from the goats.*

get off on the wrong foot

to make a bad start: *I'm going to try harder to get on with Jane's boyfriend — we seem to have got off on the wrong foot and there is always a bad atmosphere when he comes round to the flat.*

be gunning for *(someone)*

to try to find opportunities to attack or criticize (someone): *That teacher has been gunning for me since the first day of term and I don't know why.*

fall flat on one's face

to fail badly at something, especially in a humiliating way: *Jenny is always so smug and everyone hopes that one day she will fall flat on her face.*

plain sailing

progress without difficulty: *I'm looking forward to going to university but I know that it won't be all plain sailing.*

be rough on *(someone)*

to be bad luck for someone: *It was rough on James to fail his driving test when he had only made one mistake.*

run a mile

to go to great lengths to avoid someone or something: *Paul has asked me to go to the dance with him but I'd run a mile rather than go with him.*

play second fiddle to *(someone)*

to have a lower or less important position than (someone): *I was glad when Mary moved out of the flat because I always felt that I was playing second fiddle to her.*

waste one's breath

to say something which is not listened to: *Dave has often told Nick that he should study more but he is wasting his breath.*

thumb one's nose at *(someone)*

to show defiance or contempt to (someone): *Andy is thumbing his nose at the college authorities by not attending his lectures.*

Do it Yourself

1 Give an idiom which is similar in meaning to **separate the sheep from the goats**.

2 If you **get off on the wrong foot with someone** do you find that you get on very well from the moment that you meet?

3 If someone **is gunning for you** does that person wish you well?

4 Fill in an idiom to complete the sentence:

Maureen did not want to make a presentation to the whole class because she was terrified of _____.

5 If something is **plain sailing** is it very difficult to do?

6 If something **is rough on you** are you likely to feel sorry for yourself?

7 Fill in an idiom to complete the sentence:

Tom offered me a job in his butcher shop but I would sooner _____ than work there — I'm a vegetarian!

8 If you **play second fiddle to someone** do you feel superior to that person?

9 Fill in an idiom to complete the sentence:

I asked John not to drink too much at the party but somehow I feel that I was _____.

10 If you **thumb your nose at someone** are you being respectful to that person?

53 A Riding Lesson

Idioms in Context

'Do I look very **broad in the beam** in these jodhpurs?' Joan asked May. 'No, not at all,' replied May, 'but why are you wearing them?' Joan didn't look too happy and said, 'It's Alf. He **has horses on the brain** and wants to teach me horse-riding.' May was surprised, saying, 'I thought horse-riding was only for people **out of the top drawer**.' To this Joan replied, 'Apparently not. Alf's parents haven't much money, but his mother's **a leading light** in the local riding club.' 'But usually you would **go to any lengths** to avoid exercise,' said May to Joan. 'Have you **taken leave of your senses**?' 'I think I may have done,' said Joan and went to meet Alf. When they arrived at the stables, she felt rather **green about the gills** when she saw the size of the horse. She wanted to go home but thought, '**The die is cast**! I can't change my mind now.' When she got on the horse, Joan felt as though she was **taking her life in her hands** and hated every minute of her riding lesson, especially when it began to rain. Tired, wet and aching in every limb, she limped home to get into a hot bath. Later she said to May, 'That's **put the tin lid on** my relationship with Alf. I was tiring of him anyway and, after that, I don't want to see him again. And I never want to see another horse!'

Know the Meaning

broad in the beam (*informal*)
wide in the hips: *I gave away my jeans because they made me look broad in the beam.*

have (*something*) **on the brain**
to be unable to forget about something: *George has windsurfing on the brain just now — it's all he can talk about.*

out of the top drawer
from the upper social classes: *Harry doesn't want to go to university because he thinks that it is only for people out of the top drawer.*

a leading light
an important person: *Helen is a leading light in the local community.*

go to any lengths
to do something, no matter what is involved: *Peter would go to any lengths to avoid sitting his exams.*

take leave of one's senses
to become slightly mad: *You must think that I have taken leave of my senses if you think that I would give up my job to go into business with you.*

green about the gills
looking unwell, as if one were about to be sick: *Pauline looked a bit green about the gills when she got off the rollercoaster.*

the die is cast
something has been done which makes the future inevitable: *I've handed in my notice at work and so the die is cast.*

take one's life in one's hands
to take a great risk: *Anna took her life in her hands when she suggested that it was in fact the teacher that had made a mistake.*

put the tin lid on (*something*) (*informal*)
to add the last unpleasant detail to something unsatisfactory: *I failed my English exam and so that's put the lid on my chances of getting into university.*

Do it Yourself

1 If you feel that you look **broad in the beam** in an outfit do you think that it is flattering and makes you look slim?

2 If you **have something on the brain** do you have no interest in it?

3 If you are **out of the top drawer** would you describe yourself as being lower-class?

4 Fill in an idiom to complete the sentence:
Mrs Williams is a _____ in the local theatrical company — they never put on a show without her.

5 If you **go to any lengths** to do something are you prepared to put in whatever effort is required in order to do it?

6 Insert the word which is missing from the idiom:
*Colin has decided to leave university, and we all think that he has **taken** _____ **of his senses**.*

7 If you are **green about the gills** are you looking radiant and in perfect health?

8 If someone says of a situation that **the die is cast** is it possible to prevent it happening?

9 Fill in an idiom to complete the sentence:
I've agreed to go skiing with Jane on Saturday but I can't help feeling that I'm _____.

10 Insert the word which is missing from the idiom:
*One of my friends has scratched the driver's door and that's **put the** _____ **on** the chances of Dad lending me the car ever again.*

54 Dog-minding

Idioms in Context

Sam phoned his friend, Ronnie, early one Saturday morning. 'How would you like to help me look after Mr Frost's dog?' he asked. Ronnie was surprised and asked, 'Mr Frost, our teacher? Why are you **currying favour with** him?' Sam replied, 'I'm not. He's a friend of my grandmother and she'll **take umbrage** if I refuse.' Ronnie thought for a moment and then said, 'I've never looked after a dog before, but I'm not doing anything else and **variety's the spice of life**!' When Ronnie arrived and saw the size of the dog, he **changed colour**. 'What kind of dog is that?' he asked nervously. 'It seems very large.' 'It's an Irish setter,' Sam replied.' After a while they took the dog into the back garden and were kicking a ball around, when the dog suddenly leapt over the wall. 'Now **the fat's in the fire**', said Sam. 'We had better go after it. Mr Frost's going to be furious if we have to **come clean** and admit we let him escape **under our very noses**.' They ran out of the back gate and caught sight of the dog, but it would not come to them and ran away when they got close. 'That dog can go **like the clappers**,' complained Ronnie. It **led** them **a merry dance** for most of the morning but, at last, they caught it and led it home. It looked **as though butter would not melt in its mouth** when its owner arrived to collect it.

Know the Meaning

curry favour with (*someone*)

to try to gain (someone's) favour, and get him/her to like one and treat one well, by using flattery: *Sam said that he thought that my paintings were very good but I think that he was just trying to curry favour so that I would lend him some money.*

take umbrage

to feel, and show that one is offended at something that someone else has done: *I took umbrage at the way that the others decided what film we were going to see without even asking my opinion.*

variety is the spice of life

many different things can happen in life but the changes that one experiences are what makes it interesting: *Bob is taking me to a Mexican restaurant tonight — I don't know if I will like it but variety is the spice of life, after all.*

change colour

to become very pale or red in the face as a result of emotion, either fear or anger: *The teacher changed colour when she realized that the student had overheard his remarks and she was obviously very embarrassed.*

the fat is in the fire

trouble can be expected: *The fat is in the fire now that the boss knows that James went to a football match when he was supposed to be off ill.*

come clean

to tell the truth about something (often about something about which one has previously lied): *David decided it was time to come clean and admit that he had broken the vase.*

under someone's very nose

right in front of someone: *I can't believe that my wallet was stolen under my very nose — I didn't see or feel a thing.*

like the clappers (*informal*)

very fast: *The horse took off like the clappers when the shot was fired.*

lead (*someone*) **a merry dance**

to cause someone much unnecessary trouble or inconvenience, often by constantly changing one's mind or by behaving erratically: *Howard asked Tracey to marry him but she has led him a merry dance and keeps asking for more time to reach a decision.*

look as though butter wouldn't melt in one's mouth

to appear very innocent: *Wendy's son is a real hooligan, but he looks as though butter would not melt in his mouth.*

Do it Yourself

1 If you **curry flavour with** a person are you being pleasant so that he/she will treat you well?

2 Give an idiom which is similar in meaning to **take umbrage**.

3 If you feel that **variety is the spice of life** are you unwilling to try new and different things?

4 If you **change colour** are you upset about something?

5 Insert the word which is missing from the idiom:

Dad has just noticed that the window is broken — the ____ is in the fire now.

6 Give an idiom which is similar in meaning to **come clean about something**.

7 Fill in an idiom to complete the sentence:

Susan could not believe that her husband had been having an affair right _____.

8 If you go **like the clappers** do you move very slowly?

9 Insert the word which is missing from the idiom:

*The child **led** his mother **a ____ dance** by having a different favourite food each day.*

10 Insert the words which are missing from the idiom:

*I can't believe that John is the person that has been stealing from us — he **looks as though ____ wouldn't melt in his mouth**.*

55 Market Research

Idioms in Context

Rona was feeling rather nervous. Her friend, Jill, had asked her to help with a market research project for her father's firm. 'They've got a new range of cookery products **in the pipeline** and they're anxious to **get the low-down on** what people look for when they chose kitchenware,' Jill had said. Usually the firm used a team of trained market-researchers but some of these had **left** them **in the lurch** this time. Rona was not sure if she would **have the brass neck** to go round knocking at people's doors and asking them questions, but she felt it would be good experience. Also, it was something that she could add to her CV. She rather feared that people would send her away with **a flea in her ear** and wouldn't want to be interviewed. If they felt like that, she would get no information and would **have egg on her face** when she handed in her blank documents. However, she found most people helpful, although she had **played a losing game** when she had tried to conduct the research in the afternoon. Most people were at work then. One old man **bit** her **head off** and someone else threatened to get his dog to **see** her **off**, but, apart from that, she was successful in getting the required information. Rona was particularly pleased when an old lady said that a visit from such a pleasant, cheerful young lady **had made** her **day**.

Know the Meaning

in the pipeline

in preparation, but not yet ready: *Andrew heard that there was a new job in the pipeline.*

get the low-down on *(someone/something)* *(informal)*

to get information, often confidential or potentially damaging: *Magazines are always giving the low-down on celebrities' private lives.*

leave *(someone)* in the lurch

to leave someone in a difficult situation without help: *I was really left in the lurch when Debbie phoned to say that she was not able to look after the children today.*

have the brass neck *(to do something)*

to be bold and impertinent enough to do something unacceptable: *Can you believe that Sam had the brass neck to ask me if I would go to the dance with him after telling me how upset he was at Lena's refusal?*

a flea in one's ear

a sharp scolding: *If the landlord complains about the rent being late I will give him a flea in his ear for not fixing the hole in the roof.*

have egg on one's face/be left with egg all over one's face

to be left looking foolish: *William had egg on his face after the teacher asked him to tell the whole class why he was laughing.*

play a losing game

to attempt to do something in which it is obvious that one is not going to succeed: *I'm studying for my exams but I feel as though I'm playing a losing game — I don't understand a lot of the work.*

bite *(someone's)* head off

to answer (someone) sharply and angrily: *Sharon bit my head off when I told her that I had forgotten to collect her clothes from the cleaners.*

see *(someone)* off

to chase (someone) away: *That salesman came to the door last night again but I soon saw him off.*

make *(someone's)* day

to make (someone) very happy: *Getting an 'A' in my exam really made my day.*

Do it Yourself

1 Give an idiom which is similar in meaning to **in the pipeline**.

2 If you **get the low-down on** something do you feel that you know something about it?

3 Fill in an idiom to complete the sentence:

Janet was meant to be babysitting for me tonight but she just phoned and cancelled and so I'm really _____.

4 Fill in an idiom to complete the sentence:

Fraser _____ to phone and ask if he could get his job back after being fired for stealing.

5 If someone gives you **a flea in your ear** is that person displeased with you?

6 If you **have egg on your face** do you appear to be silly?

7 If you **play a losing game** are you likely to achieve your goal?

8 Insert the word which is missing from the idiom:

*I know that I'm late but there is no need to **bite my _____ off**.*

9 If you **see someone off** are you trying to get rid of that person?

10 Fill in an idiom to complete the sentence:

Betty was really happy when she received the flowers. They really _____.

56 A Wrong Diagnosis

Idioms in Context

'What's wrong with Dad these days?' asked Jim of his brother Matt. 'He's different somehow, but I can't **put my finger on** how he's changed.' 'I can't say that I have noticed anything, but then I've hardly seen Dad recently,' replied Matt. Jim went on, 'It's so easy to **rub** him **up the wrong way** these days and he's usually so placid. All of us have been having to **mind our p's and q's** all the time so as not to upset him.' Matt was concerned and said, 'I'm going to spend some time with him this evening and I'll let you know if I think anything's wrong.' Next day he said to Jim, 'Dad seems to **have the devil of a job** concentrating. I was telling him about my new course and all the information was **going in one ear and out the other**. Usually he's so interested in what we're doing,' Jim said. 'I've been thinking. The business **is on the up and up** and so that won't be worrying him. But what about his health? He **has no time for** doctors but he could have something that he thinks needs attention.' 'Let's ask him!' said Matt. When they did ask their father he laughed and said, 'I see that you've been **putting two and two together**. Fortunately you were **off the mark** completely. I've been preoccupied because I've been buying another business. Now it's **in the bag** I'll get back to normal. But thanks for your concern!'

Know the Meaning

put one's finger on (something)

to describe (something) exactly or to identify (something): *Sally put her finger on the problem when she said that we did not make enough money to employ another person.*

rub (someone) **up the wrong way**

to annoy (someone): *I don't get on with Mike — he always manages to rub me up the wrong way.*

mind one's p's and q's

to be very careful: *You should mind your p's and q's when you are talking to the manager.*

have the devil of a job (doing something)

to find something very difficult to do: *I had the devil of a job putting those shelves up.*

go in one ear and out the other

to make no impression: *I don't know why I bother telling you anything — it always goes in one ear and out the other.*

be on the up and up (informal)

to be doing very well, especially financially: *Things have been on the up and up for Simon since he took that job at the bank.*

have no time for (someone/something)

to despise (someone or something): *Pauline has no time for lawyers after she spent all that money getting divorced.*

put two and two together

to work out something: *It took me a long time but I finally put two and two together.*

off the mark

not accurate, wrong: *John thought that it would not cost much to repair his car but his estimate was way off the mark.*

in the bag (informal)

certain: *I was surprised that I did not get that job because I thought that it was in the bag.*

Do it Yourself

1 Insert the word which is missing from the idiom:

*The food is delicious but I can't quite **put my** _____ **on** what herbs you have used.*

2 If someone **rubs you up the wrong way** are you irritated?

3 If you are told to **mind your p's and q's** are you able to relax and say anything that you want to?

4 Insert the word which is missing from the idiom:

*You will **have the** _____ **of a job** getting tickets for that concert.*

5 If someone tells you something and it **goes in one ear and out the other** do you pay a great deal of attention to what has been said?

6 If things **are on the up and up** for you are you likely to be depressed?

7 If you **have no time for** something do you think that it is of little use?

8 Fill in an idiom to complete the sentence:

I _____ and realized that John had stolen the money.

9 Give an idiom which is opposite in meaning to **off the mark**.

10 If something is **in the bag** do you not know what will happen?

57 Essay Time

Idioms in Context

'We haven't been given the title of our English essay by Mr Thomson yet,' said Dave. 'It may have **slipped his mind**. Do you think we should remind him?' 'Have you **lost your marbles**?' asked Patrick in amazement. 'Don't even think about it! Just **let sleeping dogs lie**.' 'Perhaps he's **had a change of heart** about giving us another one. He does give us a lot of work to do,' suggested Mary. '**That'll be the day**!' cried Patrick. 'Mr Thomson seems to love giving students too much work.' Dave then commented, 'I don't want to write the essay, but I'd rather do it now rather than later in the term when we'll be **up to our ears in** other work.' Patrick did not agree. 'You worry too much about work. Just enjoy the extra free time and **make hay while the sun shines**!' he said. Dave and Mary and some of their fellow students went off to have some coffee. Just as they were talking about going to the cinema and trying to decide on which film to see, Patrick appeared looking extremely miserable. 'I knew that you were **tempting fate** when you mentioned the English essay, Dave. Mr Thomson's just put the choice of titles up on the notice board,' he said. 'What are they about?' asked Mary. 'Don't ask me! I **couldn't make head nor tail of** any of them. They're all **as clear as mud**!' was his reply.

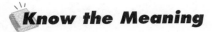

Know the Meaning

slip one's mind
to be forgotten about, usually temporarily: *I'm sorry that I did not go to the supermarket for you but it just slipped my mind.*

lose one's marbles *(informal)*
to become insane: *I'm not climbing that mountain — have you lost your marbles?*

let sleeping dogs lie
not to look for trouble on purpose, to leave things as they are: *I don't think we should remind dad about this damaged car — I think that we should just let sleeping dogs lie.*

have a change of heart
to change a decision: *Alison had a change of heart and decided to ask Peter to the party after all.*

that will be the day
that is very unlikely: *Has Greg got a job? — that'll be the day!*

up to one's ears *(something)*
deeply involved in (something): *Mary is not coming out tonight as she's up to her ears in studying for her exams.*

make hay while the sun shines
to make the most of an opportunity while it is possible to do so: *I'm starting a new job next weekend so I'm going to make hay while the sun shines until then.*

tempt fate
to act in a way which is likely to bring misfortune on oneself: *You will be tempting fate if you go out without an umbrella.*

not to be able to make head nor tail of *(something)*
to be unable to understand (something): *I can't make head nor tail of the instructions that came with the video player.*

as clear as mud
not at all clear, not easy to understand: *Claire gave me directions to get to her house but they are as clear as mud.*

Do it Yourself

1 If someone asks you to do something and it **slips your mind** do you remember to do it?

2 If people tell you that you have **lost your marbles** do they think that you are acting reasonably?

3 If you decide to **let sleeping dogs lie** are you trying to avoid trouble?

4 Insert the word which is missing from the idiom:

*I hope that you **have a _____ of heart** and decide to go to the hospital appointment.*

5 Insert the word which is missing from the idiom:

*Have I enough money to buy a flat? **That will be the _____!***

6 If you are **up to your ears** in work do you have lots of spare time?

7 If you **make hay while the sun shines** are you unable to do anything because you are worrying about the future?

8 Insert the word which is missing from the idiom:

*I don't want to _____ **fate** by choosing a name for the baby before it is born.*

9 Fill in an idiom to complete the sentence:

I read the article that was in the newspaper but I _____ of it.

10 Write down an idiom which is opposite in meaning to **as clear as mud.**

58 Forming a Band

Idioms in Context

'You know that Keith is thinking of starting a band,' said Frank to Carl. 'No, that's **news to me**,' replied Carl. 'He wants you to audition for the part of lead singer,' Frank went on. '**Hold your horses**!' cried Carl. 'If Keith wants to start a band, **more power to** his **elbow**, but it's got nothing to do with me.' Frank replied, 'Peter is also part of the band and he was supposed to contact you and **run** the idea **up the flagpole**.' 'Well, he didn't,' said Carl, 'and if he had, he would have been **wasting his breath**. I'm far too busy to be in a band and I'm not even a very good singer. In fact Keith knows that. Asking me must have been **a last-ditch effort** to find a singer. He must be desperate.' 'You're being too modest,' said Frank, 'but can you suggest anyone else? I wouldn't like to see Keith's plans for the band **go up in smoke**.' To this Carl replied, 'Anything would be better than the whole project **going off at half-cock**. But I do know someone who might take the job on. Terry was considering being a professional singer, but he was worried about not **making the grade** and so he's studying economics. He sings a lot of pop music as well as more classical stuff.' In the end Terry agreed because he thought singing with Keith's band might **pave the way for** other singing roles.

Know the Meaning

be news to (someone)

to be a piece of new information: *It is news to me that Frank has resigned.*

hold your horses

to wait for a moment, not to act hastily: *Hold your horses — I think that you should think carefully before you decide to leave university.*

more power to (someone's) **elbow**

good luck to someone: *Anne has decided to give up her job and go to her college — more power to her elbow!*

run (something) **up the flagpole**

to put forward (an idea) to see how people react to it: *I have an idea for a new product, but I'd like to run it up the flagpole at a staff meeting before I mention it to my boss.*

waste one's breath

to say something which is ignored: *I feel like I'm wasting my breath when I talk to Ian because he never takes any of my advice.*

a last-ditch effort

a final, desperate attempt to do something: *Michael cut his prices in a last-ditch effort to save his business.*

go up in smoke/go up in a puff of smoke

to disappear leaving nothing behind, to come to nothing: *It was very difficult for Fiona when her holiday plans went up in smoke.*

go off at half-cock

to be unsuccessful as a result of a lack of preparation: *The plan to throw a surprise party for Julia's birthday went off at half-cock because Stephen brought Julia along before the other guests had arrived.*

make the grade

to do as well as is required: *I hope that I make the grade when I start my new job.*

pave the way for (something)

to make it possible for (something) to happen: *The new school rules pave the way for the students to play a part in the running of the school.*

Do it Yourself

1 If someone tells you something and it is **news to you** have you been told something that you already knew?

2 If you **hold your horses** do you act immediately?

3 If you are going to do something and someone says to you '**more power to your elbow**' does that person want you to succeed?

4 Insert the word which is missing from the idiom:

*Before we make our final decision I have another suggestion that I would like to **run up the** _____.*

5 If you feel that you have **wasted your breath** saying something do you believe that people have not paid attention to what you have said?

6 Fill in an idiom to complete the sentence:

My boss offered me a raise in _____ to make me stay but I had already found another job.

7 If you make an arrangement and it **goes up in smoke** does it remain unchanged?

8 If someone tells you that an event has **gone off at half-cock** does that person think the event has been as successful as it could have been?

9 Give an idiom which is similar in meaning to **make the grade**.

10 If you **pave the way for** something are you deliberately trying to prevent it from happening?

A Mini-Dictionary of Idioms

A to Z

from A to Z very thoroughly and completely: *Anna was taught Italian cooking by her mother who knew the subject from A to Z.*

accidents

accidents will happen things can go wrong unexpectedly for anyone: *Don't worry about the car — accidents will happen and at least you were not hurt.*

account

give a good account of oneself to do well: *I hope to give a good account of myself in my next set of exams.*

OPPOSITE

not to do oneself justice not to do something as well as one could have done: *Jack wasn't feeling very well and he didn't do himself justice in the cross-country race.*

ace

within an ace of (something/doing something) very near to (something or doing something): *I was within an ace of getting an 'A' for my last essay.*

act

a hard act to follow someone or something that sets such a high standard that others will have difficulty meeting it: *They've advertised my boss's job, but she's a hard act to follow.*

get your act together to get oneself organized: *Jenny usually left doing her homework until the last minute but this year she decided to get her act together and finish it ahead of time.*

air

clear the air to make a situation less tense and difficult by talking about any problems: *There was a lot of confusion about who was responsible for what but we had a staff meeting to clear the air.*

make the air turn blue to swear strongly and profusely: *Sam really made the air turn blue when he found out that someone had stolen his car.*

walk on air/be walking on air to feel very happy: *Sheila has been walking on air since she got engaged last week.*

SIMILAR

be on cloud nine to feel very happy: *Mary and Peter have been on cloud nine since they discovered that they're going to have a baby.*

all

all in exhausted, very tired: *I can't reach the top of the hill — I'm all in.*

SIMILAR

dead on one's feet exhausted, extremely tired: *We'll all be dead on our feet by the time we've loaded the furniture van.*

be all over (someone) to be over-friendly to someone, to make too big a fuss of someone: *Wendy was really embarrassed that Fred was all over her at the party.*

angel

an angel of mercy a person who appears, bringing help, when they are particularly needed: *Derek was an angel of mercy when he said that he could lend me the money for the deposit for the holiday.*

SIMILAR

a knight in shining armour a person who brings help to someone in a difficult and not very hopeful situation: *I lost my purse and couldn't pay for my train ticket, but a knight in shining armour on the train lent me some money.*

apron-strings

tied to (someone's) apron-strings too much under the influence or control of a woman, especially one's mother or wife: *Bill's mother seems to make all his decisions for him — he's really tied to her apron-strings.*

arm

chance one's arm to take a risk: *It looks like it might rain but I think I will chance my arm and cycle to work.*

OPPOSITE

play safe/play it safe to take no risks: *Winnie is playing safe with the money which she won — she has put it in the bank.*

cost an arm and a leg (*informal*) to be very expensive: *The computer game was one that Robert had always wanted but it cost an arm and a leg.*

twist **(someone's)** arm to try to persuade (someone) to do something against his/her will, to put pressure on (someone) to do something: *Ellie seems reluctant to go to the party but, if you twist her arm, she'll probably go with you.*

be up in arms to be angry and to make a protest about something: *Ian was up in arms when he realized that the time of the test had been changed and no one had told him.*

B

back

break the back of **(something)** to complete the most difficult part of (a task): *I've got to hand my essay in tomorrow but at least I've broken the back of it.*

put **(someone's)** back up to annoy (someone): *It really put my back up when Helen started boasting about how much money she earned.*

SIMILAR

make **(someone's)** hackles rise to make (someone) angry: *People dropping litter makes the old man's hackles rise.*

the back of beyond a very remote or isolated place: *I didn't buy that house because it was in the back of beyond.*

bag

a bag of tricks all the equipment, etc needed to do something: *I hope the plumber brings his bag of tricks with him when he comes to look at the sink.*

bag and baggage with all one's belongings: *Fiona moved out of the flat, bag and baggage, without saying goodbye.*

in the bag *(informal)* certain: *I was surprised that I did not get that job because I thought that it was in the bag.*

OPPOSITE

up in the air undecided, uncertain: *Meg hasn't had her exam results yet and so her university plans are still up in the air.*

ball

on the ball alert and sharp-witted: *It will be difficult to sell your old car to Sam for more than its worth — he's really on the ball as far as cars are concerned.*

a different ball game an entirely different situation or matter: *I'm happy to lend you my bicycle, but lending you my car is a different ball game.*

OPPOSITE

the same old story a situation that occurs in the same way very frequently: *We thought that Jill would change when she went to college, but it was the same old story — she did no work and was always missing classes.*

bank

break the bank to leave someone without any money: *Maureen wanted to go on holiday to Jamaica but she realized that doing so would break the bank.*

bargepole

not touch **(someone/something)** with a bargepole to refuse to have any contact or involvement with someone or something: *I wouldn't touch that firm with a bargepole — the management treats the staff very badly.*

OPPOSITE

welcome **(someone/something)** with open arms to accept or receive (someone or something) willingly and eagerly: *Surprisingly the staff welcomed the new style of management with open arms.*

bark

his/her etc bark is worse than his/her etc bite he/she etc sounds angry and fierce, but is in fact harmless: *All the students were nervous of being put in Mr Lennon's class, but they soon found out that his bark was worse than his bite.*

bars

be behind bars be in prison: *That man should be behind bars after causing that car accident.*

SIMILAR

be inside *(informal)* to be in prison: *Apparently Roger is back home — I thought that he was still inside.*

bat

like a bat out of hell extremely quickly, very fast: *When the burglar heard the police car siren he ran out the back of the building like a bat out of hell.*

beam

broad in the beam *(informal)* wide in the hips: *I gave away my jeans because they made me look broad in the beam.*

bed

a bed of roses *(usually found in negative constructions)* a very easy and pleasant situation: *I know Sally had a tragic childhood, but mine wasn't exactly a bed of roses.*

to make one's bed and have to lie in it to have to suffer the consequences of one's own actions: *Susan ran off with a married man and is now deeply unhappy, but her mother just said that she's made her bed and she'll have to lie in it.*

belle

belle of the ball the most attractive woman or girl present at a gathering: *There were many beautiful women at the party but everyone agreed that Vicky was the belle of the ball.*

belt

tighten one's belt to economize greatly, to spend a great deal less money: *Joe and Sue have just had another child and have had to tighten their belts.*

SIMILAR

draw in one's horns to economize greatly, to spend a great deal less money: *Meg is only able to work part-time now and has really had to draw in her horns.*

berth

give (someone/something) a wide berth to avoid having contact with (someone or something): *The Wilsons advised their son to give the boy next door a wide berth — the police had arrested him on a drugs charge.*

bets

hedge one's bets to act to protect oneself against possible failure, loss, criticism, etc: *I think I'll hedge my bets and cook enough food for ten people — someone may bring a friend along.*

bill

fit the bill to be exactly what is required, to be extremely suitable: *I've been looking for a birthday present for my sister and this watch will fill the bill.*

I've been looking for some dark blue curtain material and I think that this will fit the bill.

SIMILAR

be just what the doctor ordered: to be exactly what is required: *Jenny's been feeling depressed recently and she's going on a shopping trip — she says it's just what the doctor ordered.*

foot the bill to pay (for something): *Jack applied for a bank loan to help him foot the bill for his daughter's wedding.*

SIMILAR

pick up the tab *(informal, especially American)* to pay for (something), to pay the bill for (something):

George left the restaurant hurriedly, leaving my father to pick up the tab.

bird

eat like a bird to eat very little: *I'm worried about Janice because she looks very thin and she eats like a bird.*

OPPOSITE

eat like a horse to eat a great deal: *Marcia is so fat and yet she eats like a horse.*

bit

do one's bit to do one's fair share of a task: *'We've both got full-time jobs now. It's important that you do your bit at home,' said Jean to her husband.*

SIMILAR

pull one's weight to do one's fair share of a task: *We're supposed to be working as a team to move all this furniture, but Joe is not pulling his weight.*

take the bit between one's teeth to go ahead and act on one's own without taking advice or instructions from others: *Steve was tired of waiting for the phone-call from the actors' agency and so he decided to take the bit between his teeth and phone them.*

bite

bite off more than one can chew to try to cope with more than one is capable of or to try to do something that is too difficult for one: *Mary found that she had bitten off more than she could chew when she went back to work full-time shortly after she had twins.*

'I would like to study medicine,' said Frances, 'but I don't want to bite off more than I can chew'.

blind

the blind leading the blind used to describe a situation in which one person who does not know what he/she is doing tries to help another person who is in the same state: *James is a very bad driver — when he was trying to teach Margaret to drive it was definitely the blind leading the blind.*

blood

be after (someone's) blood to have the intention of severely punishing (someone): *My boss has been after my blood since I forgot to give him an important message.*

make (someone's) blood run cold to make (someone) feel extremely frightened or horrified: *My blood ran cold as I heard the heavy footsteps behind me in the dark alley.*

blue

until one is blue in the face having made maximum effort: *I shouted until I was blue in the face but the other climbers still could not hear me.*

board

above board open and honest, without hiding anything: *I would check whether Jack's business is above board before investing any money in it if I were you.*

SIMILAR

on the level *(informal)* honest, lawful, not crooked: *The police thought the trader was selling stolen goods but apparently he's on the level.*

go by the board to be abandoned or cast aside: *Mary was meant to be on a diet, but that went by the board when she saw the chocolate cake.*

bomb

look as though a bomb had hit (something) to be in a very untidy state: *Dad's been looking for some papers in his study and the room looks as though a bomb had hit it.*

bone

a bone of contention a cause of argument: *Paul and Michelle don't get on very well these days — that car crash is still a bone of contention between them.*

books

in (someone's) bad books/ in someone's black books unpopular with (someone), out of favour with (someone): *I damaged dad's car and I'm now in his bad books.*

OPPOSITE

in (someone's) good books popular with (someone), in favour with (someone): *If you want to stay in the teacher's good books you had better hand in your work on time.*

boots

lick (someone's) boots to flatter (someone) and do everything which he/she wants: *People say that Peter got promoted because he was always licking the manager's boots.*

bottle

have the bottle to (do something): to be brave or bold enough (to do something), to have the courage (to do something): *It took a lot of bottle to admit in public that he had made a mistake.*

OPPOSITE

chicken out of (something/doing something) to lose one's nerve, not to be brave or bold enough(to do something which one said one was going to do): *Jack was going to dive from the highest level but chickened out at the last minute.*

hit the bottle *(Informal)* to begin to drink too much alcohol: *John and his friends decided that they were going to hit the bottle after their exams were finished.*

OPPOSITE

go on the wagon to stop drinking alcohol: *Jim's doctor has advised him to go on the wagon for the sake of his health.*

boy

the golden boy/girl a young man/woman who is talented and expected to do well in his/her career: *Tracey was the golden girl in her physics class.*

OPPOSITE

a black sheep a member of a group or family who is much less satisfactory than the other members: *Rob's brothers all went to university and got good jobs, but he's the black sheep — he's been unemployed for years.*

brain

have (something) on the brain to be unable to forget about something: *George has windsurfing on the brain just now — it's all he can talk about.*

SIMILAR

have a bee in one's bonnet to be unable to forget about something, to be obsessed by something: *Lily has a bee in her bonnet about complementary medicine just now.*

brainwave

have a brainwave to have a sudden good idea: *Julie was trying to think of ways to make money and had a brainwave — she would offer her services as a babysitter.*

breath

waste one's breath to say something which is ignored: *I feel like I'm wasting my breath when I talk to Ian because he never takes any of my advice.*

Dave has often told Nick that he should study more but he is wasting his breath.

breathing

be breathing down (someone's) neck to come very close to (someone), often in order to watch him/her closely or to try to make him/her go or work faster:

The driver of the car behind is breathing down my neck, but I'm not going to drive any faster in this fog. My boss is never out of my office — he's breathing down my neck for the end of year report.

bricks

be in with the bricks *(informal)* to have been in a place, organization, etc for a long time and appear to be going to stay even longer: *I can't believe the physics teacher is going to another school because we all though that she was in with the bricks.*

brush-off

give (someone) the brush-off to treat someone in an unwelcoming way in order to get rid of him/her, to reject (someone) abruptly: *I applied for a job with the new publishing firm but I got a letter back immediately giving me the brush-off.*

bull

take the bull by the horns to deal with something boldly and without delay: *Many of the staff were worried about being made redundant and so they decided to take the bull by the horns and ask for a meeting with the manager.*

SIMILAR

grasp the nettle to tackle a problem or difficult task boldly: *The boss is not keen on people taking holidays at short notice but I'll just have to grasp the nettle and ask if I can have next week off.*

bullet

bite the bullet to deal as bravely as possible with something that is unpleasant but unavoidable: *The boss valued all of his workforce, but the firm had cash problems and he had to bite the bullet and declare some of them redundant.*

get the bullet *(informal)* to be dismissed from a job, etc: *Several people got the bullet when the two firms merged.*

SIMILAR

get the axe *(informal)* to be dismissed from a job, etc: *The two firms are being merged and several of the staff will get the axe.*

bundle

be a bundle of nerves to be very nervous: *Jill is always a bundle of nerves when she has to sit an exam.*

SIMILAR

have the jitters *(informal)* to be very nervous and agitated: *Molly has the jitters — she's going for a job interview.*

burner

put (something) on the back burner to delay dealing with (something), to set (something) aside in order to attend to it later: *Their plans to move house have been put on the back burner for the moment.*

business

make it one's business (to do something) to be interested or determined enough to ensure that one does something: *Mrs Parkinson has really made it her business to find out who smashed the shop window.*

mean business to have serious intentions about something: *The boss has said that unpunctual workers will be asked to leave and he means business.*

butter

look as though butter wouldn't melt in one's mouth to appear very innocent: *Wendy's son is a real hooligan, but he looks as though butter would not melt in his mouth.*

button

press the panic button to react to an assumed difficult or dangerous situation by panicking and acting in an over-hasty or over-dramatic manner: *Don't tell Dad that Heidi is late coming home from school — he'll only press the panic button.*

bygones

let bygones be bygones to forgive and forget past disagreements, arguments, etc: *Mark and Susan went through a very bitter divorce some years ago, but they finally agreed to let bygones be bygones.*

cage

rattle (someone's) cage to upset or annoy (someone): *You look furious — who rattled your cage?*

can

carry the can *(informal)* to take the blame: *'It was your idea and so you can carry the can,' said Julie to her sister.*

OPPOSITE

get off scot free not to be punished: *Two of the robbers went to prison, but the other two got off scot free.*

in the can *(informal)* certain, agreed: *Julie says that she does not know if she passed her exam but I think it is in the can.*

canoe

paddle one's own canoe to be in control of one's own affairs without assistance from anyone else:

I know you like to paddle your own canoe but you can still ask people for advice.

SIMILAR

stand on one's (own) two feet to be independent and be in control of one's own affairs: *Fay should leave home and learn to stand on her own two feet.*

cap

put on your thinking cap to think of a way to solve a problem: *Emily realized that it was time to put on her thinking cap when she did not have enough money to pay her bills.*

cards

on the cards very likely to happen: *Some of the staff know that the closure of the firm is on the cards and are looking for other jobs*

play one's cards right to make the most of one's chances of success: *If I play my cards right at this interview I could get promoted.*

cart

put the cart before the horse to do or say things in the wrong order: *The couple have had a baby and now they're getting married — isn't that putting the cart before the horse?*

cat

let the cat out of the bag to reveal a secret, often unintentionally: *We had planned a surprise party for our parents' wedding anniversary but my sister let the cat out of the bag.*

SIMILAR

give the game/show away to reveal something that was meant to be kept secret, often unintentionally: *The child denied eating sweets but the chocolate on his chin gave the game/show away.*

like a cat on hot bricks very nervous and restless: *Jane has been like a cat on hot bricks all morning waiting for her exam results.*

catch

catch (someone) red-handed to find (someone) who is doing something wrong: *Greg had suspected that someone was taking money from the till, and then he caught Dave red-handed.*

SIMILAR

catch (someone) in the act to find (someone) who is doing something wrong: *I wouldn't have believed that the child would steal from my purse, but I caught her in the act.*

chalk

chalk it up to experience to accept something unfortunate that has happened and to try to avoid the same thing happening again: *I'm annoyed that I failed my exam, but I suppose that I'll just need to chalk it up to experience and study harder next time.*

chance

have a fighting chance to have a chance of success if great effort is made: *I want to go to university next year and my teachers think that I have a fighting chance if I study hard.*

jump at the chance to take advantage of an opportunity eagerly and without hesitation: *If Helen asked me to go on holiday with her I'd jump at the chance.*

change

have a change of heart to change a decision: *Alison had a change of heart and decided to ask Peter to the party after all.*

OPPOSITE

stick to one's guns not to change one's opinion, attitude, etc: *We all tried to persuade Paul from joining the protest group, but he stuck to his guns.*

charm

work like a charm to be very effective: *Susan had a very itchy rash but the cream, which she got from the doctor, worked like a charm.*

chase

a wild-goose chase an attempt to do something that has no chance of success: *Paul spent a long time looking for the old castle, but it turned out to be a wild-goose chase — it was destroyed by fire years ago.*

chickens

chickens come home to roost used to describe a situation in which past errors or misdeeds committed by someone begin to have an adverse effect on him/her, sometimes after quite a long time: *Mr Bruce would like to live with one of his children now that he is old, but he was a very uncaring father and all of them have refused — his chickens have come home to roost.*

chin

keep one's chin up not to get discouraged or lose hope in a difficult situation. *The doctor said that it is quite a serious illness but that I should keep my chin up.*

SIMILAR

keep one's pecker up *(informal)* not to get discouraged or lose hope in a difficult situation.

choice

Hobson's choice the choice between taking what is on offer or getting nothing: *I said that I would be delighted to go to the dance with Michael but really it was Hobson's choice — everyone else already had a partner.*

clappers

like the clappers *(informal)* very fast: *The horse took off like the clappers when the shot was fired.*

clean

come clean to tell the truth about something, especially to admit that you have done something wrong, to confess: *You might as well come clean — our neighbour saw you break the window.*

SIMILAR

make a clean breast of it/something to tell the truth about something you have done wrong, to confess to something: *It was you who lost your sister's brooch and you should make a clean breast of it. If you make a clean breast of your crimes the judge might treat you more leniently.*

clockwork

like clockwork smoothly, without any problems: *Everything went like clockwork on the day of the wedding.*

clue

not to have a clue about (something) to know nothing or very little about (something), to be ignorant about (something): *Jeff is brilliant at English and history but he doesn't have a clue about maths.*

OPPOSITE

be clued up on (something) *(informal)* to be knowledgeable about (something): *Jill's really clued up on Shakespeare and she would help you with your essay.*

coast

the coast is clear there is no longer any danger or difficulty present: *The burglars watched everyone leave the building and broke in when the coast was clear.*

cobwebs

blow the cobwebs away to stop oneself from feeling tired and sluggish, often by going out in the fresh air: *I'm going for a walk along the seafront to blow the cobwebs away.*

colour

change colour to become very pale or red in the face as a result of emotion, either fear or anger: *The teacher changed colour when she realized that the student had overheard her remarks and she was obviously very embarrassed.*

with flying colours very easily and successfully: *Anne came through the job interview with flying colours.*

come

come clean to tell the truth about something (often about something about which one has previously lied): *David decided it was time to come clean and admit that he had broken the vase.*

SIMILAR

make a clean breast of (something) to admit or confess to (something), often something that one has previously denied: *At first Beth denied losing the book, but then she decided to make a clean breast of it.*

coop

fly the coop *(informal)* to leave home: *Now that all her children have flown the coop Madge has started on a university course.*

corner

just around the corner very near in time, soon: *I'm buying presents — Christmas is just around the corner.*

courage

pluck up courage/screw up one's courage to force oneself to do something, although one might be feeling afraid or unwilling: *The junior clerk finally plucked up courage/screwed up his courage and asked his boss for a wage rise.*

OPPOSITE

lose one's bottle *(informal)* to lose one's courage, not to have the courage to do something: *Peter was going to jump from the window but at the last minute he lost his bottle.*

crack

at crack of dawn very early in the morning: *We'll have to leave home at crack of dawn to catch the first bus.*

cracks

paper over the cracks to pretend that everything is all right and problem-free when this is not the case: *Meg and Terry have separated after years of quarrelling although they tried to paper over the cracks for the sake of their children.*

crawling

be crawling with to be overrun with, to be full of: *The town is crawling with tourists now. Don't go into the kitchen because it's crawling with ants!*

cropper

come a cropper *(informal)* to suffer misfortune: *Billy came a cropper when he was driving his brother's motorbike.*

cup

not **(someone's) cup of tea** not something that (someone) likes or prefers: *I won't come swimming with you because it's not really my cup of tea.*

daggers

at **daggers drawn** ready to start fighting or quarrelling at any minute: *Tricia and Brian have been at daggers drawn ever since their divorce.*

daisy

as **fresh as a daisy** very bright and lively: *I slept really well last night and woke up this morning feeling as fresh as a daisy.*

SIMILAR

bright-eyed and bushy-tailed very bright and lively: *We were all exhausted after the long car journey, but our young daughter was bright-eyed and bushy-tailed.*

damper

put a **damper on (someone/something)** to lessen the enjoyment or enthusiasm of (someone or something): *We were having a wonderful time at the party when one of our friends took ill — and that put a damper on the evening.*

dance

lead **(someone) a merry dance** to cause someone much unnecessary trouble or inconvenience, often by constantly changing one's mind or by behaving erratically: *Howard asked Tracey to marry him but she has led him a merry dance and keeps asking for more time to reach a decision.*

date

go on a **blind date** to go out with someone that one has not previously met, usually in the hope that romance develops: *Stella doesn't have a boyfriend just now and Terry has arranged for her to go on a blind date with a man who works in his office.*

day

call it a **day** to decide or declare that something has come to an end: *Dad has been working at the same firm for thirty years but he has decided to call it a day and do something else.*

carry the day to gain victory: *'We may be missing our best player but we can still carry the day if we play as well as we can,' said the coach to his team.*

make **(someone's) day** to make (someone) very happy: *Getting an 'A' in my exam really made my day.*

that **will be the day** that is very unlikely: *Has Greg got a job? — that'll be the day!*

his/her/its etc days are numbered the end of someone or something is imminent: *I think that I will have to get a new car soon, because my old one's days are numbered.*

dead

dead set on (something/doing something) determined or very anxious to get or do (something): *Joe is dead set on going to university but he will have to get good enough marks in his school exams.*

death

dice with death *(sometimes used humorously)* to risk putting oneself in great danger or getting into serious trouble: *Those racing drivers look as though they're dicing with death. I'll be dicing with death if I ask my father for another loan.*

hang on like grim death to take a very firm hold of something in a difficult situation: *The instructor told me to hang on like grim death while she fetched a ladder.*

decks

clear the decks to tidy up and remove unnecessary items in preparation for starting a task: *Before James began to make the Christmas dinner he decided to clear the decks.*

departure

a **new departure** a change, something completely different: *It's a new departure for the café to sell evening meals, but it seems to be doing well.*

depth

out of one's **depth** in a situation which one cannot cope with, often because of lack of knowledge, skill, etc: *Pete joined the college chess club but he was completely out of his depth — he is only a beginner and the others are all experienced players.*

devil

have the **devil of a job (doing something)** to find something very difficult to do: *I had the devil of a job putting those shelves up.*

die

the **die is cast** something has been done which makes the future inevitable: *I've handed in my notice at work and so the die is cast.*

differences

patch up differences to end an argument or quarrel by trying to forget about or ignore what caused it in order to remain friendly: *Margo and Billy are always arguing but they agreed to patch up their differences because they're both good friends of Molly.*

sink (our, your, their, etc) differences to forget about past disagreements and try to get on with each other: *If we are going to be living in the same flat, I think that we should sink our differences and try to be friends.*

direction

point (someone) in the right direction to show (someone) what to do, to help (someone) get started on (something): *Tom's father wants to buy a computer but he knows very little about them — he's hoping that Tom will point him in the right direction.*

ditchwater

as dull as ditchwater extremely dull or uninteresting: *The lecture was as dull as ditchwater and so we left early.*

dodo

as dead as a dodo completely dead or no longer useful, fashionable, popular, etc: *I thought that flared trousers were as dead as a dodo, but I see that they are back in fashion.*

dogs

let sleeping dogs lie not to look for trouble on purpose, to leave things as they are: *I don't think we should remind dad about this damaged car — I think that we should just let sleeping dogs lie.*

donkey

donkey work the difficult and unrewarding part of a task: *Donald is so lazy and he always gets someone else to do the donkey work for him.*

door

at death's door on the point of dying, often used as an exaggeration: *There was no way that I could have gone into work yesterday — I had flu and was at death's door.*

doorstep

on one's own doorstep very near to where one lives: *I expect that the burglar comes from another town — I don't think that someone would break into houses on their own doorstep.*

doubting

a doubting Thomas a person who does not believe something: *Don't be a doubting Thomas — I'm sure that Matt will pay you back the money.*

down

have a down on (someone) to be very hostile or opposed to someone: *I'm not surprised that I got a low mark for my history essay because the teacher has always had a down on me.*

SIMILAR

have it in for (someone) to be very hostile to (someone) and try to do harm to (him/her): *Linda's had it in for Martin ever since his brother stopped going out with her sister.*

drain

laugh like a drain to laugh loudly: *I find it really embarrassing going out with Claire — she laughs like a drain and people always stare at her.*

drawer

out of the top drawer from the upper social classes: *Harry doesn't want to go to university because he thinks that it is only for people out of the top drawer.*

dream

go like a dream to perform or progress very well and smoothly: *Peter was delighted with his new motorbike because it went like a dream.*

drop

a drop in the bucket a very small part of the amount that is needed: *Susan said that she could afford help in the shop one day a week, but that is really only a drop in the bucket.*

SIMILAR

a drop in the ocean a very small part of the amount that is needed: *We launched an appeal for money to repair the church roof but what we received was just a drop in the ocean.*

drop into (someone's) lap to be obtained without effort: *You can't expect a good job to just drop into you lap — you'll have to get out and look for one.*

ready to drop (informal) very tired, exhausted: *I've had a terrible day at work and I'm ready to drop.*

dust

like gold dust extremely rare: *The band is very popular and tickets for tonight's concert are like gold dust.*

dying

be dying for (something/to do something) (informal) to want (something) very much: *I ran all the way home and now I'm dying for a drink.*

E

ear

bend (someone's) ear to talk a great deal about (something) to (someone), although he/she might not want to listen: *I try to avoid Jenny because she's always bending my ear about how successful her children are.*

go in one ear and out the other to make no impression: *I don't know why I bother telling you anything — it always goes in one ear and out the other.*

grin from ear to ear to smile broadly, to look very pleased or happy: *The coach of the local football team was grinning from ear to ear when they won the cup.*

SIMILAR

be all smiles to have a smiling face, to look very pleased or happy: *The bride and groom were all smiles as they left the wedding reception.*

SIMILAR

grin like a Cheshire cat to smile broadly as though very pleased with oneself: *Kit was grinning like a Cheshire cat when he beat his rival in the tennis match.*

make a pig's ear of (something) *(informal)* to do (something) very badly: *Phil baked a cake for Caroline's birthday, but he made a pig's ear of it and had to buy one from the baker instead.*

SIMILAR

make a hash of (something) *(informal)* to do (something) very badly, to make a mess of (something): *I tried to ice the cake, but I made a hash of it.*

play it by ear to do something without making any fixed plans beforehand: *I haven't thought of what I'm going to say to the committee — I'm just going to play it by ear.*

turn a deaf ear to (something) to refuse to listen to or pay attention to (something): *The workers pleaded with the boss to give them more money but he turned a deaf ear to their request.*

OPPOSITE

be all ears to listen with great attention: *Tell me exactly what you want me to do — I'm all ears.*

my etc ears are burning someone elsewhere is talking about me, usually unkindly: *Rob's ears should have been burning last night — Meg and Jane were discussing how handsome he is.*

up to one's ears in (something) deeply involved in (something): *Mary is not coming out tonight as she's up to her ears in studying for her exams.*

earth

run (someone/something) to earth to find (someone/something) after a long search: *I finally ran Peter to earth in the gym after looking for him all evening.*

edge

on edge uneasy, apprehensive: *Joseph was on edge all day waiting for his exam results to arrive.*

effort

a last-ditch effort a final, desperate attempt to do something: *Michael cut his prices in a last-ditch effort to save his business.*

egg

have egg on one's face/be left with egg all over one's face to be left looking foolish: *William had egg on his face after the teacher asked him to tell the whole class why he was laughing.*

put all one's eggs in one basket to depend totally on the success of one particular plan: *I would not put all my eggs in one basket if I were you — you should interview several people for the job.*

element

in one's element in a situation that one finds comfortable and pleasant: *Frank was in his element when they started talking about politics.*

OPPOSITE

out of one's depth in a situation with which one cannot deal: *Simon claims to know quite a lot about politics, but he was out of his depth when Alan and Ros were discussing the election.*

end

come to/reach the end of the road to reach the end of some kind of relationship or association: *Matt has been friends with Rickie since they were at school, but he decided that their friendship had come to the end of the road when Rickie asked his girlfriend out on a date.*

expense

spare no expense to spend whatever sum of money it takes to get what one wants without worrying about the cost of this: *Our neighbours spared no expense on their anniversary party — they had several crates of the best vintage champagne.*

eyes

cry one's eyes out to weep bitterly: *When I got the letter about failing my exams I cried my eyes out.*

face

fall flat on one's face to fail badly at something, especially in a humiliating way: *Jenny is always so smug and everyone hopes that one day she will fall flat on her face.*

have a face like a fiddle to look unhappy: *Fred had a face like a fiddle when he read his exam results — he must have done badly.*

have a long face to look sad or disapproving: *Sam had a long face when I told him that I had changed my mind about going to the party with him.*

put a brave face on it/put on a brave face to try to appear calm, confident, happy, etc when one has no cause to feel like this: *Rose was very disappointed at losing the tennis match but she put a brave face on it as she left the court.*

SIMILAR
put on a bold front to try to appear confident when one is feeling nervous or uncertain: *Sue was terrified at the idea of singing in public but she put on a bold front.*

put a good face on it to pretend to be happy or satisfied when this is not the case: *Carol's putting a good face on it but she is really upset about breaking up with James.*

show one's face to appear somewhere where one is unwelcome, especially when doing so should make one feel embarrassed or ashamed: *I can't believe that Julie had the nerve to show her face at Sandra's birthday party after the way she criticized her last week.*

fall

fall foul of (someone/something) to get into a situation where someone/something is angry with one or hostile to one, to get into trouble with (someone/something): *Jane fell foul of her boss when he found out that she had been late for work every day last week. Jack fell foul of the new speed restrictions and was charged by the police.*

falling

be falling to bits to be in a very bad state of repair, to be torn or broken: *Jack tried to sell me a car but you could see that it was falling to bits.*

SIMILAR
be falling to pieces: to be in a very bad state of repair, to be torn or broken: *We badly need some new kitchen chairs — these are falling to bits.*

fate

seal the fate of (someone/something) to ensure that something, usually unpleasant, happens (to someone or something) in the future: *Laura knew that being late for work one more time would seal the fate of her chances of promotion.*

tempt fate to act in a way which is likely to bring misfortune on oneself: *You will be tempting fate if you go out without an umbrella.*

favour

curry favour with (someone) to try to gain (someone's) favour, and get him/her to like one and treat one well, by using flattery: *Sam said that he thought that my paintings were very good but I think that he was just trying to curry favour so that I would lend him some money.*

SIMILAR
lick (someone's) boots to flatter (someone) and do everything that he/she wants: *No one but you believes that Tim got top marks because he licks the teacher's boots.*

feathers

ruffle (someone's) feathers to upset or annoy (someone): *I don't know what is wrong with Kati, but something has certainly ruffled her feathers.*

SIMILAR
rattle (someone's) cage to upset or annoy (someone): *Someone must have rattled Debbie's cage — she looks very angry.*

feeling

have a sinking feeling to have a feeling of pessimism or dread about a forthcoming event: *I have a sinking feeling that I am going to fail my exams.*

feet

be rushed off one's feet to be extremely busy with no time to rest: *The restaurant was crowded and all the waiters were rushed off their feet.*

OPPOSITE
twiddle one's thumbs to do nothing, to be idle: *All the other students have holiday jobs but Sally is sitting at home twiddling her thumbs.*

dead on one's feet (*informal*) totally exhausted: *By the end of the party I was dead on my feet.*

have two left feet to be clumsy or awkward, especially in dancing: *John refuses to come to the disco because he says that he has two left feet and couldn't ask any girl to dance with him.*

stand on one's own two feet to be independent, not to rely much on other people: *June relies too much on her family — she should leave home and learn to stand on her own two feet.*

fences

mend fences to put things right after an argument or disagreement: *I suppose that I should go and see her and try to mend fences.*

OPPOSITE

make waves to cause trouble: *Most of the class is well-behaved, but one child delights in making waves.*

rush one's fences to act in haste without care: *I should have found out more about the job before applying — I always tend to rush my fences.*

OPPOSITE

take one's time not to hurry, to be slow and careful: *Don't take the first job which you are offered — take your time and find something which really suits you.*

fiddle

on the fiddle *(informal)* making money dishonestly: *The manager had to sack the company accountant after she found out that he had been on the fiddle.*

play second fiddle to (someone) to have a lower or less important position than (someone): *I was glad when Mary moved out of the flat because I always felt that I was playing second fiddle to her.*

field

play the field to spread one's interests, affections, etc widely rather than concentrating on any one subject or person, especially to have a great many partners of the opposite sex, rather than just one: *I'm in no hurry to settle down and get married — I want to play the field while I'm still young.*

fight

be spoiling for a fight to be eager to have a fight or quarrel, to be in an argumentative mood: *I'd stay away from Helen if I were you — she's in a foul mood and I think she's spoiling for a fight.*

pick a fight with (someone) to start a quarrel or argument quite deliberately with (someone): *It's best to avoid Rob when he's been drinking — he usually picks a fight with someone.*

finger

have (someone) wrapped/wound/twisted round one's little finger: to be able to persuade (someone) to act exactly as one wishes: *If we all want more time to finish the essay we should get Emma to ask the teacher — she has him wrapped round her little finger.*

put one's finger on (something) to describe (something) exactly or to identify (something): *Sally put her finger on the problem when she said that we did not make enough money to employ another person.*

all fingers and thumbs awkward, clumsy at doing something with one's hands: *Jean tried her best to sew the hem of her skirt, but she was all fingers and thumbs.*

get one's fingers burnt to suffer as a result of action which one has taken: *I don't lend anyone money because I've had my fingers burnt too many times before.*

have green fingers to be good at gardening: *Tracey has got green fingers — her garden always looks beautiful.*

keep one's finger on the pulse to keep oneself informed about current ideas, events, etc: *The manager at the clothes shop is really good; she keeps her finger on the pulse and always manages to get the latest fashions in store before other shops.*

fire

hang fire to delay or to be delayed: *Our plans to build a conservatory are hanging fire until we have some more money.*

the fat is in the fire trouble can be expected: *The fat is in the fire now that the boss knows that James went to a football match when he was supposed to be off ill.*

SIMILAR

the balloon has gone up trouble is about to start: *The balloon has gone up — my father has found out that I crashed his car.*

fish

have other fish to fry to have something else to do: *Jim asked me to go clubbing, but I have other fish to fry — I'm going to the cinema with Colin.*

OPPOSITE

be at a loose end to have nothing to do: *I'm busy but Jack's at a loose end — he might help you.*

like a fish out of water in a situation to which one is unaccustomed and which makes one feel uncomfortable: *Rose's new boyfriend and his friends are all keen on sport and she hates it — she's a real fish out of water when they all get together.*

there are plenty more fish in the sea a saying meaning that, although one opportunity may have been lost, there are many more likely to arise, often used to someone who has just ended a relationship to reassure him/her that there are many more women/men in the world who could be potential partners: *Don't cry because Paul's left you — he wasn't really your type and there are plenty more fish in the sea.*

SIMILAR

there are plenty more **pebbles on the beach** a saying meaning the same as **there are plenty more fish in the sea**: *When his fiancée went off with one of his fellow-students, Sean didn't find it helpful that so many people said to him, 'There are plenty more pebbles on the beach.'*

fit

have a fit *(informal)* to become very angry: *Mr Smith will have a fit if he sees that dog digging up his garden.*

SIMILAR

fly off the handle suddenly to become very angry, to lose one's temper: *It's difficult to discuss anything with Jane — if you disagree with her she just flies off the handle.*

flagpole

run **(something)** up the flagpole to put forward (an idea)to see how people react to it: *I have an idea for a new product, but I'd like to run it up the flagpole at a staff meeting before I mention it to my boss.*

flat

that's flat that is final, there is to be no more discussion or argument: *I'm not lending you my car and that's flat!*

flavour

flavour of the month a thing or person that is particularly liked by someone at the moment: *Computer games are flavour of the month with children at school.*

flea

a flea in one's ear a sharp scolding: *If the landlord complains about the rent being late I will give him a flea in his ear for not fixing the hole in the roof.*

SIMILAR

a ticking-off a scolding, often a mild one: *I got a ticking-off from my mother for breaking her favourite vase.*

fling

have a final fling to enjoy a last chance of extravagance or indulgence before one's circumstances change: *Sarah is getting married next week and she wants to have a girls' night out on Saturday so that she can have a final fling before she settles down.*

floor

wipe the floor with **(someone)** to defeat (someone) completely: *Tom will wipe the floor with Bill in the golf tournament.*

fly

a fly in the ointment something that spoils a situation: *The only fly in the ointment is that I will have to miss the party in order to go to the concert.*

he/she etc would not hurt a fly he/she etc is very gentle: *I don't believe that the nursery school teacher smacked the unruly child — she wouldn't hurt a fly.*

I etc would like to be a fly on the wall I etc would like to be present at a situation without being seen so that it is possible to hear what is said without being involved: *I would like to be a fly on the wall when James finds out that Rachel crashed his car.*

foam

foam at the mouth to be very angry: *Dad was foaming at the mouth when I told him that I had forgotten to put petrol in the car.*

fool

playing the fool to act in a silly way, especially to amuse other people: *James did not do well at school because he was usually too busy playing the fool to listen to the teachers.*

foot

get off on the wrong foot to make a bad start: *I'm going to try harder to get on with Jane's boyfriend — we seem to have got off on the wrong foot and there is always a bad atmosphere when he comes round to the flat.*

have one foot in the grave to be near death, especially because of old age, usually used as an exaggeration: *I don't think that Mr Jones should be in charge of the football team — he's got one foot in the grave.*

fort

hold the fort to take temporary charge of a job, task, etc: *George was babysitting for his sister, but he asked Fred to hold the fort while he went to the supermarket.*

fruit

bear fruit to produce results: *I have a feeling that his plan may bear fruit after all.*

game

play a losing game to attempt to do something in which it is obvious that one is not going to succeed:

I'm studying for my exams but I feel as though I'm playing a losing game — I don't understand a lot of the work.

the game is not worth the candle the project is not worth the effort, time, etc spent on it: *I did think it was a good idea to hold a charity jumble sale, but we made so little money that the game was not worth the candle.*

get

get carried away to be so enthusiastic about something that one stops behaving sensibly or loses self-control: *Amy always gets carried away when she's planning a party and spends far too much money.*

OPPOSITE
keep one's cool to remain calm and self-controlled: *Jody was losing the tennis match but she kept her cool and won in the end.*

get lost a rude way of telling someone to go away: *'I've told you that I don't want to see you — so get lost!' said Phil.*

get lumbered with (someone/something) (informal) to be given an unwanted or unpleasant task or responsibility: *I got lumbered with paying for the meal for everyone because no one else had brought enough money.*

get round to (something/doing something) to do (something) after a period of delay or postponement: *When John finally decided to ask Joanna for a date, she was going out with someone else.*

ghost

not have the ghost of a chance not to have any chance of success: *David wants to go out with Jane but he doesn't have the ghost of a chance.*

gift

have the gift of the gab to have the ability to speak fluently and articulately: *Paul could talk his way out of anything — he's really got the gift of the gab.*

OPPOSITE
be a person of few words to be the kind of person who says as little as possible, only saying what is strictly necessary: *Rona's father is a person of few words, but her mother is very chatty.*

gills

green about the gills looking unwell, as if one were about to be sick: *Pauline looked a bit green about the gills when she got off the rollercoaster.*

give

give as good as one gets to be as successful as one's opponent in an argument, fight, etc: *Sharon was the school bully who was used to winning arguments, but the new student gave as good as she got.*

go

be on the go to be active or busy: *My friend has two little boys and they're on the go all day — they're so exhausting!*

go out with (someone) to have a regular romantic relationship with (someone), usually someone of the opposite sex, to date (someone) on a regular basis: *Matt and Libby have been going out with each other for several years but they don't live together.*

SIMILAR
go steady with (someone) to have a regular romantic relationship with (someone): *Rena is not going steady with Jim — they're just friends.*

SIMILAR
be seeing (someone) to have a regular romantic relationship with (someone): *Phil and Diane were engaged but he discovered that she had been seeing someone else.*

go to sleep (of a limb) to feel numb: *My foot went to sleep during the long car journey.*

have a go at (something) to make an attempt at (something), to try to do (something): *I'm going to have a go at cutting down this old tree.*

SIMILAR
try one's hand at (something) to make an attempt at (something), to try to do (something): *Nora is going to try her hand at baking.*

make a go of (something) to make a success of (something): *Karen has really made a go of her restaurant — it's always full.*

good

be up to no good to be doing something wrong or illegal: *I don't want to go out tonight and leave the children on their own — I think that they will be up to no good.*

goose

cook (someone's) goose to ruin (someone's) chances of success completely: *Being late for the audition really cooked Mike's goose — he now has no chance of getting a part in the play.*

gooseberry

play gooseberry to be in the company of two other people, usually two people who are in love with each other, who do not wish you to be there: *Paul and Suzanne asked me to go to the pictures with them, but I didn't fancy playing gooseberry.*

grabs

up for grabs (*informal*) ready to be taken, bought, etc: *The house next door is up for grabs — do you think that you might be interested?*

grade

make the grade to do as well as is required: *I hope that I make the grade when I start my new job.*

SIMILAR

pass muster to meet a required standard, to be accepted as being good enough: *A great many people have applied for entrance to the university, but not all of them will pass muster.*

grain

go against the grain in opposition to a natural inclination: *It goes against the grain for Sharon to say no to a cream cake.*

grass

let the grass grow under one's feet to waste time: *Paula's got a new job already and she only handed in her notice last week — she certainly doesn't let the grass grow under her feet.*

grip

lose one's grip to lose control or understanding of something: *The manger was under a great deal of stress and it was obvious he was losing his grip.*

ground

get (something) off the ground to get (something) started and operating successfully: *We're trying to start a new tennis club but we'll never get it off the ground without more members.*

SIMILAR

get (something) up and running to get (something) started and operating successfully: *The scientist does not have the money to get his research project up and running.*

shift one's ground to change one's opinions: *Ron and Ken are having a political argument, and Ken has begun to shift his ground a little.*

SIMILAR

do a U-turn to change one's opinions or policy, to reverse a course of action: *The club had a men-only policy, but they did a U-turn and admitted women members.*

stand one's ground to refuse to give in: *I've decided that I'm not going to go to university and I'm going to stand my ground, whatever my parents say.*

OPPOSITE

throw in the towel to give up, to give in, to admit defeat: *We formed a protest group against the new building development, but we had to throw in the towel after a few months.*

suit (someone) down to the ground to suit (someone) extremely well, to be exactly right for (someone): *Jim loves travelling and so that job will suit him down to the ground.*

SIMILAR

suit (someone) to a T to suit (someone) extremely well, to be exactly right for (someone): *A small flat in that area would suit me down to a T.*

gunning

be gunning for (someone) to try to find opportunities to attack or criticize (someone): *That teacher has been gunning for me since the first day of term and I don't know why.*

SIMILAR

have one's knife in (someone) to be very hostile to (someone) and try to do harm to (him/her): *I'm not surprised that the marketing manager has left the firm — the managing director has been having his knife in him for some time.*

guns

go great guns to be doing very well, to be very successful: *I had difficulty with this essay at first, but now it's going great guns.*

SIMILAR

make great strides to make good progress: *Ella didn't do very well in junior school, but she's made great strides since she went to senior school.*

H

hackles

make (someone's) hackles rise to make someone angry: *Every time I think about that man stealing my purse, it makes my hackles rise.*

hair

keep one's hair on *(informal)* to stay calm: *Keep your hair on — there's only a tiny scratch on your car's paintwork.*

OPPOSITE

fly off the handle to become very angry: *Colin's very quick-tempered — he flies off the handle if you disagree with him.*

let one's hair down to relax and enjoy oneself: *Our boss is always very formal in the office but she really lets her hair down at parties.*

make (someone's) hair stand on end to terrify or horrify (someone): *That horror film we watched last night made my hair stand on end.*

SIMILAR

make (someone's) blood run cold to terrify or horrify (someone): *The newspaper description of the murder made my blood run cold.*

half-cock

go off at half-cock to be unsuccessful as a result of a lack of preparation: *The plan to throw a surprise party for Julia's birthday went off at half-cock because Stephen brought Julia along before the other guests had arrived.*

halfway

meet (someone) halfway to reach an agreement with (someone) by which you each agree to some of the other's demands in return for having yours accepted, to reach a compromise with (someone): *Harriet wanted to work freelance at home, but the firm wanted someone to work full time in the office and so they decided to meet each other halfway — Harriet was to work part of the week at home and part of the week in the office.*

hammer

go at it hammer and tongs to have a fierce argument or row: *We had a dreadful journey — Anne and Bert were going at it hammer and tongs all the time about who was the better driver.*

SIMILAR

be at each other's throats to have a fierce argument or row, to quarrel violently: *I am not surprised to hear that Tim and Sara have separated — every time I met them they were at each other's throats.*

hand

cap in hand humbly: *Fraser went to his wife cap in hand and asked her to forgive him.*

live from hand to mouth to have enough money to supply only what is really needed for survival, to be very poor: *Both parents are unemployed and the family are living from hand to mouth.*

the iron hand in the velvet glove ruthlessness or firmness disguised by apparent softness: *Don't be fooled by that teacher — she may seem easygoing but I can assure you it is a case of the iron hand in the velvet glove.*

throw in one's hand to abandon a plan, course of action, etc: *Julie had hoped to go to university, but she decided to throw in her hand when she failed her final school exams.*

try one's hand at (something) to see if one can do (something), to attempt to do (something): *I have never made a cake before, but I will try my hand at it.*

SIMILAR

have a stab at (something) to try to do (something): *I'll have a stab at winning the golf tournament.*

all hands to the pumps everyone must do what he/she can to help, especially in a crisis situation: *Granny is coming home from hospital tomorrow so it will be all hands to the pumps to help her settle in.*

win hands down to win very easily: *I don't like playing tennis with Jane — she always wins hands down.*

hang

get the hang of (something) to begin to understand how to (do something): *I think I'm finally getting the hang of driving.*

hash

make a hash of (something) *(informal)* to do (something) badly, to make a mess of (something): *I tried to make a delicious meal for everyone but I made a hash of it and had to get a take-away instead.*

SIMILAR

make a pig's ear of (something) *(informal)* to do something very badly: *Helen tried to mend the tear in her dress, but she made a pig's ear of the repair.*

hat

a hat-trick an action done successfully three times in a row: *The crowd cheered with delight as William scored his hat-trick.*

hatchet

bury the hatchet to agree to stop quarrelling or fighting and be friends again: *The Thomsons quarrelled with their neighbour over parking places, but they buried* *the hatchet when their daughter started going out with their neighbour's son.*

have

have **(someone)** on to try to get (someone) to believe something that is not true, to tease (someone): *You're having me on — I don't believe Fiona's going out with Ben because they've absolutely nothing in common!*

have **(something)** taped to have a full knowledge and understanding of (something): *My grandfather had difficulty learning to use a computer at first, but he seems to have got it taped now.*

havoc

play havoc with **(something)** to cause a great deal of damage to (something), to ruin (something): *Heavy rain played havoc with the tennis championships this year.*

hay

hit the hay/sack *(informal)* to go to bed: *I'm going to hit the hay — I've got to get up early in the morning.*

make hay while the sun shines to make the most of an opportunity while it is possible to do so: *I'm starting a new job next weekend so I'm going to make hay while the sun shines until then.*

SIMILAR

strike while the iron is hot to act while a situation is favourable to one: *The bank is offering cheap loans to students this month — I think I'll strike while the iron is hot and apply for one.*

head

above one's head too difficult for one to understand: *Susan explained how to use the computer but I have to confess that it was all above my head.*

bite **(someone's)** head off to answer (someone) sharply and angrily: *Sharon bit my head off when I told her that I had forgotten to collect her clothes from the cleaners.*

head over heels completely, totally: *Pamela has fallen head over heels in love with Dave.*

laugh one's head off to laugh loudly or heartily: *Mark laughed his head off when his rival fell off his bike.*

OPPOSITE

cry one's eyes out to shed a great many tears, to weep bitterly: *The little girl cried her eyes out when her dog was run over.*

need one's head examined to be foolish or crazy: *Denise needs her head examined for taking Andy back after the way he behaved.*

SIMILAR

be round the bend *(informal)* to be crazy: *Flo must be round the bend to lend Phil her car — he's a terrible driver.*

not to be able to make head nor tail of **(something)** to be unable to understand (something): *I can't make head nor tail of the instructions that came with the video player.*

on your etc **(own)** head be it you etc will take responsibility for any negative outcome resulting from your actions, wishes, etc: *I warned Julie that Pete is a rogue — on her own head be it if she decides to marry him.*

put heads together to discuss something: *We're putting our heads together to see if we can find a way to get enough money to start a new club.*

heart

have one's heart in one's mouth to be very anxious and nervous: *We had our hearts in our mouths as the ghostly shape came towards us.*

have one's heart in the right place to have a kind, generous nature although this might not always be obvious: *Nora sometimes criticizes unemployed people but her heart's in the right place — she helps out at a hostel for homeless people.*

put new heart into **(someone/something)** to give renewed hope and encouragement to (someone or something): *Passing her exams has put new heart into Rebecca and she has decided to stay on at university.*

set one's heart on **(something)** to be very keen to get or do (something), to want (something) very much: *Jan has set her heart on studying medicine. The child had set his heart on a trip to the seaside.*

heaven

in seventh heaven extremely happy or pleased, delighted: *The young mother was in seventh heaven when she held her newborn baby.*

SIMILAR

over the moon extremely happy or pleased, delighted: *Jack was over the moon when he won a trip overseas in a holiday competition.*

hedge

look as though one had been dragged through a hedge backwards to look very untidy: *I thought that you were going to make an effort to look nice for the wedding, but you look as though you've been dragged through a hedge backwards.*

OPPOSITE
look as though one has stepped out of a bandbox to look very neat and elegant: *Janice is going for a job interview and she looks as though she has stepped out of a bandbox.*

heels

dig in one's heels /dig one's heels in stubbornly to refuse to agree to something, allow something, etc: *We hoped to persuade Judy to change her mind when she refused to join us, but she dug her heels in.*

herring

packed like herring in a barrel very tightly packed, crowded together closely: *The passengers on the bus were packed like herring in a barrel.*

hold

to hold (something) against (someone) to dislike (someone)or to think badly of (someone) because one knows that that person has done something wrong: *I know that Ruth went off with my boyfriend, but I don't hold it against her —I blame him.*

home

bring home the bacon to do something successfully, especially to earn enough money to support one's family: *Debbie's father looks after the house and her mother brings home the bacon. My boss said that I would get a salary increase if I bring home the bacon on this deal.*

feel at home to feel very relaxed as if one is in one's own home: *I knew it was the perfect house for me to buy because I felt at home from the moment I walked in.*

hop

catch (someone) on the hop to meet or find (someone) when he/she is not prepared: *Our parents certainly caught us on the hop — they came back early from holiday and we hadn't cleaned the house.*

hope

hope against hope to go on hoping that something will happen when there is no reason to believe that it will: *The family were hoping against hope that the emergency operation on their mother would be successful.*

horse

a dark horse a person about whose talents, abilities, etc little is known: *Jane has entered the talent show but she is rather a dark horse and we don't know how she's likely to perform.*

flog a dead horse to waste time on a subject or action that is no longer likely to produce successful results: *Trying to get a financial contribution from Mark is flogging a dead horse — he's just been declared bankrupt.*

look a gift horse in the mouth to criticize or complain about something which has been given to one: *You shouldn't complain about the job which your uncle found for you in his factory — jobs are scarce and you shouldn't look a gift horse in the mouth.*

you can take a horse to the water but you can't make it drink you can encourage someone to something, but you cannot force someone to do something which he/she does not want to do: *I showed Tara the library but she refused to take out any books — you can take a horse to the water, but you can't make it drink.*

change horses in mid-stream to change one's decisions, plans, etc in the middle of a project: *Frank has been studying History for a year but he wants to change horses in mid-stream and study Philosophy.*

hold your horses to wait for a moment, not to act hastily: *Hold your horses — I think that you should think carefully before you decide to leave university.*

OPPOSITE
rush one's fences to act too hastily, without taking enough care: *Give the bank manager time to study your business plan — don't rush your fences by ringing him today.*

wild horses wouldn't get/drag (one) to (do something) nothing could persuade (one) to (do something): *Rick's terrified of flying — wild horses wouldn't drag him on a plane.*

hour

put off the evil hour to postpone something unpleasant: *I suppose that I should open my exam results now — there's no point in putting off the evil hour any longer.*

the (wee) small hours very early in the morning: *It was the wee small hours before Isobel finished writing her essay. The ball did not finish until the small hours.*

hum

hum and haw to express uncertainty and be unable to come to a decision: *Dave eventually had to offer the job to someone else because Julie kept humming and hawing and would not make a decision.*

I

influence

under the influence drunk: *I would not let him drive me home because he was under the influence.*

OPPOSITE

as sober as a judge not at all drunk: *Will had only one glass of wine and was as sober as a judge.*

iron

strike while the iron is hot to act while the situation is favourable: *My boss was really pleased with me today and so I decided to strike while the iron was hot and ask for a pay rise.*

itching

be itching to (do something) to be very eager to (do something): *I was itching to tell Steve the good news, but I had been told to keep it secret.*

J

Jack Robinson

before you can say Jack Robinson very quickly: *I expect that Joanne will agree to marry Ian before you can say Jack Robinson.*

SIMILAR

in the twinkling of an eye very quickly: *They all got together and tidied the room in the twinkling of an eye.*

jewel

the jewel in the crown the most valuable or important part of something: *We had a lovely holiday but the jewel in the crown was our visit to Rome.*

job

a Job's comforter a person who attempts to be reassuring but whose comments and suggestions often makes things worse: *Dad tried to make me feel better about failing my driving test, but he was just a Job's comforter when he said that many people fail several times.*

have a job *(informal)* to have difficulty in doing something: *You'll have a job getting Peter to pay you back.*

K

kettle

a different kettle of fish something completely different: *I quite like singing around the house, but singing in public is a different kettle of fish.*

SIMILAR

a whole new ball game *(informal)* something completely different to what has gone before: *Marketing is a whole new ball game now that so many people buy things through the Internet.*

kibosh

put the kibosh on (something) *(informal)* to prevent something from being done or from being successful: *I had been planning on driving down to visit some friends in the country, but bad weather put the kibosh on my trip.*

kite

as high as a kite very excited: *The children were high as a kite when they were told that they were going to the zoo.*

OPPOSITE

as calm as a cucumber very calm and composed, not at all excited: *Madge remained as calm as a cucumber when she was told that she had won the prize.*

knife

have one's knife in (someone) to be very hostile towards (someone) and try to do harm to (him/her): *Joan's boss has his knife in her because she defeated his daughter in the firm's golf tournament.*

SIMILAR

have it in for (someone) to be very hostile to (someone) and try to do harm to (him/her).

knot

tie the knot to get married: *Liz and Bill are going to tie the knot in the local registry office, not in church.*

SIMILAR

get hitched *(informal)* to get married: *We were all amazed when Joe said that he was getting hitched — we all thought that he was a confirmed bachelor.*

know

in the know having information known only to a small group of people: *Only those in the know had any idea that George was going to a new job.*

not to know **(someone)** from Adam not to recognize (someone), not to know who someone is: *That man said hello to me but I don't know him from Adam.*

lamb

like a lamb to the slaughter meeting danger or difficulty quietly and without resistance: *Tom went into the exam room like a lamb to the slaughter.*

land

see how the land lies to consider the conditions which exist before making a decision: *I think that I will look for a new job next year, but I will see how the land lies in my present job first.*

lane

the fast lane a competitive and highly pressured way of life: *Frank decided that he had had enough of the fast lane and retired to a country cottage.*

lap

in the lap of the gods a situation that is left to chance, the outcome of which is hard to predict: *I've studied hard — the results of my exams are in the lap of the gods now.*

OPPOSITE
in the bag *(informal)* certain, sure: *Jim felt that he had done well in his school exams and that his university place was in the bag.*

leaf

turn over a new leaf to begin to behave well after a period of bad behaviour: *The child was very badly behaved in school at first but after a few weeks he has turned over a new leaf.*

league

be not in the same league as **(someone)** to be not as good at something as (someone), or not as important as (someone): *Miriam is quite a good violinist, but she is not in the same league as her sister who plays with one of the national orchestras.*

leave

take leave of one's senses to become slightly mad: *You must think that I have taken leave of my senses if you think that I would give up my job to go into business with you.*

leg

not to have a leg to stand on to have no way of excusing or defending one's behaviour: *Debbie is hoping Steve will forgive her for going out with his friend, but she does not have a leg to stand on.*

stretch one's legs to walk about after sitting or lying down for a while, to go for a walk: *We have to change planes at London and we'll have time to stretch our legs.*

lengths

go to any lengths to do something, no matter what is involved: *Peter would go to any lengths to avoid sitting his exams.*

lid

flip one's lid *(informal)* to become very angry: *Don't tell Dad that I crashed the car or he will flip his lid.*

put the tin lid on **(something)** *(informal)* to add the last unpleasant detail to something unsatisfactory: *I failed my English exam and so that's put the lid on my chances of getting into university.*

lie

lie low to stay quiet or hidden, to avoid drawing attention to oneself: *The police think that the bank robbers are lying low somewhere. Their mother was in a bad mood and so the children were lying low.*

SIMILAR
be in hiding to go somewhere where you will not easily be found, perhaps because you are in danger or because the police are looking for you: *The president of the state has gone into hiding because terrorists have threatened to kill him.*

life

lead a charmed life to continuously escape from danger or harm with no ill effect: *Elaine leads such a charmed life — she's always late, but the boss never notices.*

take one's life in one's hands to take a great risk: *Anna took her life in her hands when she suggested that it was in fact the teacher that had made a mistake.*

light

a leading light an important person: *Helen is a leading light in the local community.*

get the green light to receive permission to begin doing something: *Richard got the green light from his bank to go ahead with buying the house.*

OPPOSITE

get the red light not to receive permission to do something: *We had hoped to build an extension to our house, but we got the red light from the planning department.*

hide one's light under a bushel not to draw attention to one's talent or ability: *Richard is a very good painter but he tends to hide his light under a bushel.*

OPPOSITE

blow one's own trumpet to boast about one's talents or abilities: *Adam is a very good tennis player but people dislike the fact that he's always blowing his own trumpet.*

line

take the line of least resistance to take the course of action which will cause the least effort, trouble, etc: *I'm completely opposed to Tina's political ideas, but I couldn't be bothered arguing with her — I took the line of least resistance and kept quiet.*

read between the lines to understand more than is actually written or spoken: *Paul did not say why he was leaving but, reading between the lines, I think that he and Jane had a big argument.*

load

be a load/weight off one's mind to be a relief from something that has been worrying one: *Josh had taken out a bank loan as a student and it was a load off his mind when he was able to pay it off.*

loom

loom large to be about to happen and so to be very important: *I'll have to book more driving lessons because my test is looming large.*

lorry

fall off a lorry/fall off the back of a lorry to have been obtained by dishonest or illegal means: *Jan's brother is selling cheap video recorders, but she's worried in case they fell off a lorry.*

losses

cut one's losses to decide not to waste more time, effort, etc on something one has already spent time, effort, etc on: *I'm in the middle of a course of golf lessons but I don't enjoy the game and so I've decided to cut my losses and give it up.*

low-down

get the low-down on (someone/something) *(informal)* to get information, often confidential or potentially damaging: *Magazines are always giving the low-down on celebrities' private lives.*

lurch

leave (someone) in the lurch to leave someone in a difficult situation without help: *I was really left in the lurch when Debbie phoned to say that she was not able to look after the children today.*

make

make oneself scarce to get out of the way quickly, usually to avoid trouble or difficulty: *The students were demonstrating against high fees but they made themselves scarce when the police arrived.*

marbles

lose one's marbles *(informal)* to become insane: *I'm not climbing that mountain — have you lost your marbles?*

march

steal a march on (someone) to gain an advantage over (someone), especially by doing something earlier than he/she can do: *Jim was going to ask Anne for a date, but Peter stole a march on him and asked her out first.*

mark

off the mark not accurate, wrong: *John thought that it would not cost much to repair his car but his estimate was way off the mark.*

OPPOSITE

spot on *(informal)* absolutely accurate: *In the quiz all Becky's answers were spot on.*

quick off the mark acting in a prompt or speedy manner: *If Gillian wants to get that job she will have to be quick off the mark with her application.*

up to the mark up to the normal standard: *The restaurant used to be very good, but the meal cooked by the new chef was not quite up to the mark.*

memory

have a memory like a sieve to be very forgetful: *Jenny asked Frank to get her prescription from the chemist, but he has a memory like a sieve and forgot about it.*

OPPOSITE

have a memory like an elephant to have an extremely good memory: *Molly has a memory like an elephant — she hasn't forgotten that Jim told lies about her several years ago.*

mend

on the mend getting better: *June has been off work with the flu but she is on the mend now.*

mickey

take the mickey out of (someone) to make fun of (someone), to tease (someone), to ridicule (someone): *The new teacher is very inexperienced and the students are always taking the mickey out of him.*

mile

run a mile to go to great lengths to avoid someone or something: *Paul has asked me to go to the dance with him but I'd run a mile rather than go with him.*

mind

keep an open mind to be willing to listen to or accept new ideas: *I don't usually like that sort of thing, but I'll try to keep an open mind*

slip one's mind to be forgotten about, usually temporarily: *I'm sorry that I did not go to the supermarket for you but it just slipped my mind.*

something is preying on one's mind something is causing one constant unhappiness or distress: *Colin could not sleep at night because his forthcoming exam's preying on his mind.*

take (someone's/one's) mind off (something) to turn (someone's/one's) attention away from (something): *I'm going to go to the cinema tonight because I've got my driving test tomorrow and I want to take my mind off it.*

be in two minds about (something) to be unable to come to a decision about (something): *Fred has been offered a job but it is out of town and he is in two minds about accepting it.*

SIMILAR

hum and haw: to be unable to come to a decision about something and to express doubts: *I don't know why Paul is humming and hawing about going on the trip — it sounds marvellous.*

minute

not to have a minute to call one's own to be very busy working and to have very little time for rest or leisure: *I'm sorry that I haven't phoned you but I've not had a moment to call my own since my boss resigned.*

money

be rolling in money *(informal)* to have a great deal of money, to be very rich: *You would have to be rolling in money to be able to afford a house in that part of town.*

SIMILAR

have money to burn to have a great deal of money so that one can afford to be extravagant: *Peter and Jenny go abroad on holiday several times a year — they have money to burn.*

money is no object money is not important: *Money is no object as far as my health is concerned.*

monster

the green-eyed monster jealousy: *Sally said that she did not like my dress, but I think she was influenced by the green-eyed monster.*

more

the more the merrier the more people there are the better: *I am only expecting a few people to come to the party but everyone is welcome — the more the merrier.*

motions

go through the motions (of something/doing something) to pretend (to do something): *I was at work today but I could not concentrate — I was really just going through the motions.*

mouse

as poor as a church mouse very poor, having very little money: *He's a wealthy surgeon now but he was as poor as a church mouse when he was a medical student.*

mouth

be all mouth and trousers to tend to talk a great deal but do very little: *The teacher threatened to expel me but he is all mouth and trousers.*

down in the mouth miserable or depressed: *Sara seems rather down in the mouth — did she fail the English test?*

SIMILAR

down in the dumps *(informal)* miserable, depressed: *Joe's down in the dumps because his girlfriend's gone on holiday without him.*

move

get a move on *(informal)* to move more quickly, to hurry: *If you don't get a move on, we'll not be able to complete the project.*

SIMILAR

get cracking *(informal)* to move more quickly, to hurry: *We'd better get cracking — if we don't leave now we'll miss the train.*

SIMILAR

step on it *(informal)*: *Tell Jim to step on it — he's still at breakfast and we have to leave in ten minutes.*

movers

movers and shakers energetic and powerful people who make changes or get things done: *Dianne is excited about her business lunch with the movers and shakers from that big law firm.*

mud

as clear as mud not at all clear, not easy to understand: *Claire gave me directions to get to her house but they are as clear as mud.*

OPPOSITE
crystal clear extremely clear, easy to understand: *Elsie gave us directions and they were crystal clear.*

music

be music to (someone's) ears to please (someone) very much: *It was music to my ears when James told me that I had passed my exam.*

face the music to confront the outcome of your actions: *Mrs Thomson is at the front door asking about her broken window — I suppose that it is time to face the music and admit responsibility.*

nail

hit the nail on the head to be absolutely accurate or exact: *My father hit the nail on the head when he said that Jack was a villain.*

SIMILAR
put one's finger on it to describe something exactly, to be absolutely right or accurate about (something): *You put your finger on it when you said that Anne is a troublemaker.*

neck

have the brass neck (to do something) to be bold and impertinent enough to do something unacceptable: *Can you believe that Sam had the brass neck to ask me if I would go to the dance with him after telling me how upset he was at Lena's refusal?*

risk their necks to take a serious risk, to risk putting oneself in danger or getting into serious trouble: *You shouldn't have risked your neck going back into the burning house to get your jewellery. Pete risked his neck by asking the boss not to sack Bill for being late.*

nettle

grasp the nettle to tackle a problem or difficult task boldly: *Ned wasn't looking forward to telling his parents that he had failed his exams, but he decided to grasp the nettle that evening.*

SIMILAR
take the bull by the horns to deal with something boldly and without delay: *There's no point in waiting to see if the firm is going to close — we should take the bull by the horns and ask the boss now.*

news

be news to (someone) to be a piece of new information: *It is news to me that Frank has resigned.*

nick

in the nick of time at the last possible moment, just before it is too late: *The ambulance got there in the nick of time — the accident victim nearly died.*

SIMILAR
at the eleventh hour at the last possible minute, just before it is too late: *The workers had called a strike but at the eleventh hour management agreed to meet their demands.*

nines

be dressed to the nines to be dressed in formal, smart clothes, sometimes over-dressed: *Jane usually wears jeans and a sweater and hates parties where everyone is dressed to the nines.*

SIMILAR
be dressed to kill to be dressed in extremely smart clothes, often with the intention of attracting attention: *It's an informal party but Liz is dressed to kill — she's hoping to meet a new man.*

nose

have a nose for (something) to be good at discovering things: *Listen to Roger's plan — he always has a nose for a way to make money from nothing.*

keep one's/someone's nose to the grindstone to work very hard without stopping or make (someone) work very hard without stopping: *I'll have to keep my nose to the grindstone if I'm going to finish painting this room this evening. The new teacher believes in keeping her pupils' noses to the grindstone and always gives them lots of homework.*

keep your nose clean (*informal*) to keep out of trouble by not behaving badly: *'If you don't want to end up in prison you had better keep your nose clean,' said the police officer to Fred.*

thumb one's nose at (someone) to show defiance or contempt to (someone): *Andy is thumbing his nose at the college authorities by not attending his lectures.*

turn one's nose up **(at something)** to treat (something) with contempt, to indicate that (something) is not good enough for one: *Martin's new girlfriend turned her nose up when he suggested staying in a youth hostel — she is used to luxurious hotels.*

under someone's very nose right in front of someone: *I can't believe that my wallet was stolen under my very nose — I didn't see or feel a thing.*

nothing

for nothing without payment: *We did all that gardening for nothing — the old man didn't give us a penny.*

nothing to it very easy: *'Come on, you can jump across the river — there is nothing to it!'*

there is nothing else for it there is only one thing to do, there is no choice: *When Mark's car broke down several miles from the town there was nothing else for it — he had to walk.*

notice

sit up and take notice suddenly to start paying attention and being aware of what is going on: *We all thought that Mick was the least successful member of the family, but we sat up and took notice when he made enough money to buy a chain of shops.*

odds

make no odds to be of no importance: *It makes no odds to me if Sheila leaves town — I hardly ever see her now, anyway.*

over the odds more than necessary: *I'm really annoyed because I've just found out that I paid over the odds for my car.*

oil

burn the midnight oil to study or work until very late at night: *I'll be burning the midnight oil from now until the exams.*

pour oil on troubled waters to try to calm and soothe a person or a situation: *I tried to pour oil on troubled waters by explaining how the accident happened.*

olive

an olive branch a sign of a desire for peace: *I decided to hold out an olive branch to James and ask him to go out for a drink.*

once-over

give **(something)** the once-over *(informal)* to examine something very quickly: *Robert asked his uncle to give the car the once-over before he bought it.*

SIMILAR

take a dekko at **(someone/something)** (informal) to take a quick look at (something): *I can't afford to buy the car, but I'd like to take a dekko at it, anyhow.*

oracle

work the oracle to produce the desired result: *Rosie's studying worked the oracle and she did very well in her exams.*

order

a tall order something that is very difficult to do: *Paul wanted to complete the return journey in one day, but he knew it was a tall order.*

OPPOSITE

a piece of cake *(informal)* something that is very easy to do: *The students all thought that the exam was a piece of cake.*

give **(someone)** his/her marching orders to dismiss (someone) from a job, etc: *I had to give Jim his marching orders after I realized that he had stolen the money from the till.*

SIMILAR

give **(someone)** the sack to dismiss (someone) from a job, etc: *If you don't do the job properly the boss will give you the sack.*

own

come into one's own to have the chance to show one's best qualities, skills, etc: *When Shirley got a chance to sing in public she really came into her own although she was usually very reserved.*

p's and q's

mind one's p's and q's to be very careful: *You should mind your p's and q's when you are talking to the manager.*

pace

stay the pace to maintain progress at the same rate as others: *I've decided that I'm going to run the marathon next year since my coach thinks that I've got what it takes to stay the pace.*

show one's paces to show what one can do: *Helen is really looking forward to the talent show because she thinks it will be a good chance for her to show her paces.*

packet

make a packet (*informal*) to earn or make a great deal of money: *Jack's father made a packet when the horse won, but he lost it all on the next race.*

SIMILAR

make a mint (*informal*) to earn or make a great deal of money: *Marcus got into the computer games market early and has made a mint.*

par

below par not as healthy or well as usual: *Lucy has left work early feeling ill — she's been below par all morning.*

parting

reach the parting of the ways to end a relationship or association of some kind: *Millie and Jane have been business partners for several years, but they have reached the parting of the ways and they are both starting their own separate firms.*

patch

strike a bad patch to experience a period of difficulty or a time in which there are many problems: *The computing firm struck a bad patch, but it is now very successful once again.*

patience

have the patience of Job to be extremely patient: *You would have to have the patience of Job to teach in that school.*

SIMILAR

have the patience of a saint to be extremely patient: *You need to have the patience of a saint in order to teach young children.*

peanuts

pay (someone) peanuts to pay (someone) very little money: *Adam has a job washing dishes in a restaurant and he's being paid peanuts.*

OPPOSITE

pay (someone) a fortune to pay (someone) a great deal of money: *Martin's father's paid a fortune as head of the corporation.*

peas

look like two peas in a pod to look very much alike: *The two girls must be sisters — they look like two peas in a pod.*

SIMILAR

be the spitting image of (someone) to look very much like (someone): *The little boy is the spitting image of his grandfather.*

peeping

a peeping Tom a man who secretly watches people (often women getting undressed) through windows: *Jane reported the peeping Tom to the local police when she saw him at her bedroom window.*

penny

earn an honest penny to earn money in a honest way: *Teaching may be hard work but at least I earn an honest penny.*

not to have a penny to one's name to be extremely poor: *The groom is very rich but the bride doesn't have a penny to her name.*

pick

pick up where you had left off to continue to do something after a period of not doing so, often to start communicating with someone after a period of not doing so: *I hardly ever see my friend in Canada, but, whenever we meet, we just pick up where we left off. Sheila wants to go back to work, but she can't just pick up where she left off — she'll have to go on a re-training course.*

pie

pie in the sky hope of success or achievement which has very little or no chance of being fulfilled: *Steve thinks that he is going to become a famous actor, but that is just pie in the sky.*

piece

a nasty piece of work a very unpleasant person: *Dave warned me that the new manager is a nasty piece of work and he was right.*

a piece of cake (*informal*) something very easy or simple to do: *The first exam was a piece of cake but the others were very difficult.*

pig

bleed like a pig to bleed a great deal: *Gary cut his hand badly when laying floor tiles and was bleeding like a pig.*

sweat like a pig to sweat a great deal: *Brian was sweating like a pig after running for the bus.*

pigs might fly an expression used to indicate that something is extremely unlikely to happen: *Mike says that he is saving up to buy a car — pigs might fly!*

pinch

at a pinch if it becomes absolutely necessary, in an emergency: *At a pinch we could get four people in the back seat of the car, but it would be uncomfortable.*

SIMILAR

if it comes to the pinch if it is absolutely necessary, in an emergency: *We really only have accommodation for four guests but if it comes to the pinch we could take six.*

take (something) with a pinch of salt to have doubts about (something), to doubt that (something) is completely true: *Mary says that she is never going to be late again, but you can take that with a pinch of salt.*

pipeline

in the pipeline in preparation, but not yet ready: *Andrew heard that there was a new job in the pipeline.*

SIMILAR

on the stocks still being prepared or arranged: *I hear that a merger between the firms is on the stocks, but the details are still being worked out.*

pistol

hold a pistol to (someone's) head to force (someone) to do as one wishes, often by making threats: *My parents think that I should study more, and they're holding a pistol to my head by threatening to reduce my allowance.*

pitch

pitch in *(informal)* to begin to do something or to participate in something, especially with enthusiasm: *The party will be a success if we all pitch in and make arrangements.*

play

play it cool to deal with a problem or situation in a calm way: *Paula really wanted the job but she managed to play it cool in the interview.*

OPPOSITE

press the panic button to act in an assumed difficult or dangerous situation by panicking and acting in an over-hasty or over-dramatic way: *Don't ask Sonia to babysit — she presses the panic button when the slightest thing goes wrong.*

play safe/play it safe to act with care and caution, not to take risks: *It doesn't look as though it will rain, but I'm going to play it safe and take an umbrella.*

plunge

take the plunge to take decisive action although this may be risky or difficult, especially after hesitating for some time: *Frank has been thinking of getting married for years and now he's taken the plunge and asked Peggy to be his wife.*

pot

the pot calling the kettle black used to describe someone who is criticizing another person for doing something that he/she also does: *Pauline shouted at me for being late this morning but that's the pot calling the kettle black — she is never on time.*

pound

have one's pound of flesh to get everything that one is entitled to, even if it causes difficulties or unhappiness for others: *My job pays well but my boss expects to get his pound of flesh from me.*

power

more power to (someone's) elbow good luck to someone: *Anne has decided to give up her job and go to her college — more power to her elbow!*

practice

be out of practice to not have had a lot of practice recently: *Jill asked me to go skating with her but I'm worried that I will fall because I am out of practice.*

premium

at a premium in great demand and therefore difficult to get: *The band playing at the concert was very popular and tickets were at a premium.*

SIMILAR

like gold dust very rare and therefore difficult to get: *My favourite conductor was appearing with the local orchestra, but tickets were like gold dust.*

price

a give-away price a very cheap price, a bargain: *Let's go to the computer shop — I was told they had games at a give-away price.*

pup

sell (someone) a pup to cheat (someone), to sell (someone) something that is useless: *I realized that I had been sold a pup when the computer would not turn on.*

pushing

be pushing (a certain age) *(informal)* to be nearly a certain age: *David's granny is amazing — she's pushing 90 but she still works in her shop every day.*

question

pop the question (*informal*) to ask someone to marry you, to propose to someone: *Mary is longing to get married and hopes that her boyfriend will pop the question soon.*

the burning question a question that is of great interest to many people: *Of course the burning question is who will win the election?*

rabbit

pull a rabbit out of a hat to produce a very pleasant surprise or to achieve something unexpected: *Peter thinks that his business will have to close unless the bank manager can pull a rabbit out of a hat.*

rags

glad rags (*informal*) one's best, smartest clothes worn for parties, etc: *Now that the exams are over, it's time to put on our glad rags and celebrate.*

SIMILAR

one's Sunday best one's best, smartest clothes: *This suit is my Sunday best — I'm going to a funeral.*

rake

as thin as a rake very thin: *I don't think that Julie should go on a diet because she's as thin as a rake already.*

rally

rally round to come together for a joint effort or action, usually in a supportive way: *Ruth will be able to get out of hospital tomorrow if we all rally round and make sure that the house is ready for her.*

red

in the red in debt, (of a bank account) overdrawn: *May is highly paid and yet her account's in the red at the end of every month.*

OPPOSITE

in the black in credit, not in debt, making a profit: *The firm was in financial difficulties last year but it's in the black now.*

retreat

beat a hasty retreat to go away very quickly: *Paul beat a hasty retreat before his father could ask him to wash the car.*

OPPOSITE

stay put to remain where one is: *Pat knew that Jo wanted her to go away for some reason but she stayed put.*

ride

take (someone) for a ride to deceive or cheat (someone): *Madge was told that the second-hand washing machine was in working order, but she was taken for a ride*

SIMILAR

put one across (someone) to deceive or cheat someone: *Emma put one across me when she persuaded me to buy her camera — it needed a very expensive repair.*

rise

rise and shine an instruction to someone to get out of bed — usually in the morning: *'Rise and shine — it's a beautiful day!' shouted Peter's mother.*

river

sell (someone) down the river to betray (someone): *The workforce felt that their trade union had sold them down the river by accepting a lower wage rate from management than had originally been asked for.*

roof

hit the roof to become extremely angry: *Mother will hit the roof when she sees the stain on the new carpet.*

SIMILAR

see red to become extremely angry: *Jim always sees red when anyone criticizes his work.*

room

room to swing a cat (*usually in negative statements*) a very small amount of space: *The holiday was great, apart from the fact that the hotel room was so small there was barely room to swing a cat.*

rope

show (someone) the ropes to explain or demonstrate (to someone) how to do something: *My boss is leaving me in charge when she goes on holiday but she has promised to show me the ropes before she goes.*

rope (someone) in (for something/to do something) to persuade (someone) to join in (doing something), often when he/she might be rather reluctant: *Joan is trying to rope people in to take part in a charity walk.*

rough

be rough on (someone) to be bad luck for someone: *It was rough on James to fail his driving test when he had only made one mistake.*

Rubicon

cross the Rubicon to do something which commits one to a particular course of action without allowing one to reverse one's decision: *Jane felt that she had crossed the Rubicon after she had said that she would buy the house.*

run

in the long run eventually, in the end, after a long period of time: *It is hard having no money as a student but studying is worth it in the long run — you will get a better-paid job.*

S

sailing

plain sailing progress without difficulty: *I'm looking forward to going to university but I know that it won't be all plain sailing.*

salt

the salt of the earth a very good and worthy person: *Rita spends all her spare time helping the homeless — she really is the salt of the earth.*

say

you can say that again you are absolutely right: *Jock came in and said that the weather was dreadful and we all replied, 'You can say that again!'*

scratch

come up to scratch to do as well as is required, to reach an acceptable standard: *Kevin is nervous about going to university — he's worried that he won't come up to scratch.*

see

see (someone) off to chase (someone) away: *That salesman came to the door last night again but I soon saw him off.*

see the last of (someone/something) to see (someone or something) for the last time, not to see (someone or something) again: *Susan said, 'I'm glad to see the last of this place,' as she closed the door of the house which she had just sold.*

sense

lull (someone) into a false sense of security to lead someone to believe that everything is all right, safe, easy, etc when it is not: *Jim told Esther that her tournament opponent was not a good tennis player but he was lulling her into a false sense of security because her opponent is last year's champion.*

sewn

sewn up entirely settled or arranged: *Dave was really surprised that he did not get the job because he had thought that it was all sewn up.*

shadow

cast a shadow on (someone/something) to make (someone or something) less happy: *The fact that the bride's grandmother was ill cast a shadow over the wedding.*

shape

lick (someone/something) into shape to get (someone or something) into an orderly or efficient state: *I expect that the new boss will want to lick the staff into shape right away.*

sheep

separate the sheep from the goats to separate or distinguish the good from the bad or the worthless: *The teacher has said that she is going to give us a test next week and that she expects that it will separate the sheep from the goats.*

SIMILAR

separate the wheat from the chaff to separate or distinguish the good from the bad or the worthless: *The teacher hopes that the English test will separate the wheat from the chaff.*

sheet

as white as a sheet very pale in the face, usually because of fear or illness: *Tom looked as white as a sheet when he found out that he had failed his exams.*

SIMILAR

as white as a ghost very pale in the face, usually because of fear or illness: *Tess has been seasick and looks as white as a ghost.*

shell

come out of one's shell to become less shy: *Sara was very shy when she went to school, but she soon came out of her shell when she got to know the other children.*

shine

take a shine to (someone/something) *(informal)* to become fond of (someone or something): *I think that Bert has taken a shine to Julie — he keeps looking at her.*

ship

spoil the ship for a hap'orth o' tar to spoil something of value by trying to cut costs and not doing something very small which would improve it: *Brian insisted on ordering a bottle of expensive wine to have with the meal — he said that he did not want to spoil the ship for a hap'orth of tar.*

shoes

shake in one's shoes to be very nervous or scared: *We were shaking in our shoes when the policeman started to question us.*

shoestring

be living on a shoestring to have very little money to live on: *The young mother is living on a shoestring and cannot afford to buy sweets for her children.*

SIMILAR

pinch and scrape: to have very little money to live on: *Tom has given up his college course and taken a job — he's tired of having to pinch and scrape all the time.*

shot

give it one's best shot to try one's hardest: *You might not get the job but you've got an interview, and it's worth giving it your best shot.*

like a shot very willingly or eagerly: *I would go on holiday with you like a shot but I've arranged to go away with my family then.*

call the shots to be in control, to be in charge and make decisions: *It seems to be his deputy, and not the president, who's calling the shots now.*

shoulder

give (someone) the cold shoulder to ignore (someone) deliberately: *I saw John in the supermarket but I just gave him the cold shoulder — he treated my friend very badly.*

rub shoulders with (someone) to associate with (someone), to come into contact with (someone): *At the Youth Camp our students rubbed shoulders with students from all over the world.*

show

run the show to be in control or charge of something: *I feel much happier about the holiday now that Suzie is running the show because she's a very good organizer.*

SIMILAR

be at the helm to be in charge of something: *The school needs someone new at the helm if educational standards are going to improve.*

side

look on the bright side to be hopeful and look for the best in a situation, to be optimistic: *It may be raining but look on the bright side — the flowers are getting watered.*

OPPOSITE

fear the worst to expect a situation to have the worst possible outcome, to be pessimisitic: *Bert had just received his exam results, and his parent feared the worst when they saw his sad expression.*

take sides to support a particular person, group, etc against another, not to remain neutral: *Jim and his twin sister are always arguing but their elder brother refuses to take sides.*

sight

set one's sights on (something) to try to get (something): *I hope that the dress I have set my sights on is my size.*

sitting

be sitting pretty to be in a fortunate or favourable situation: *The local football team is sitting pretty at the top of the league.*

sixes

at sixes and sevens in confusion, in a muddle, in a disorganized state: *The students are all going home today and the place is at sixes and sevens.*

OPPOSITE

in apple-pie order neat and tidy with everything in its correct place: *Mother says that my room's a mess and that she wants to see it in apple-pie order by this evening.*

size

that's about the size of it that is an accurate assessment of a situation: *Donald thinks that he has failed his test and that seems to be about the size of it.*

skates

get your skates on *(informal)* to hurry up: *We had better get our skates on if we are going to catch the 6.30 train.*

smoke

go up in smoke/go up in a puff of smoke to disappear leaving nothing behind, to come to nothing: *It was very difficult for Fiona when her holiday plans went up in smoke.*

snowed

be snowed under with (someone/something) to be overwhelmed with (someone or something), to have a great deal of (people or things) to cope with: *The village has been snowed under with tourists all summer. The students are snowed under with essays this term.*

something

have something on to be busy, to have another engagement: *I would love to come to the party but I've got something on this Saturday.*

like something out of the ark very old-fashioned: *My mother lent me a dress to wear to the party, but I can't possibly wear it — it's like something out of the ark.*

sorrows

drown one's sorrows to drink alcohol in order to forget one's problems: *It is no use drowning your sorrows — the problem will still be there in the morning.*

sort

not a bad sort *(informal)* quite a pleasant person: *The new head teacher seems not a bad sort.*

soup

in the soup *(informal)* in serious trouble: *Jane is really in the soup after crashing her sister's car.*

SIMILAR
in hot water *(informal)* in trouble: *You'll be in hot water if you miss another day at college.*

spade

call a spade a spade to say exactly and plainly what one means: *James is very frank — he always calls a spade a spade.*

spanner

throw a spanner in the works to prevent something from happening, to spoil or ruin something: *We had the trip all planned and then Mick threw a spanner in the works by saying that he couldn't lend us his car after all.*

spirit

be with (someone) in spirit to be thinking of (someone), although not actually with him/her: *I can't come into the exam room with you, but I'll be with you in spirit.*

spot

have a soft spot for (someone/something): to be fond of (someone or something): *Edith's always had a soft spot for spaniels.*

OPPOSITE
have no time for (someone or something) to dislike (someone or something) very much: *Eddie has no time for lazy people.*

stab

have a stab at (something) to try to do (something), to have an attempt at (something): *I've never been ice-skating before but I'll have a stab at it.*

stable

lock the stable door after the horse has bolted to take action which is too late: *The Wilsons fitted a burglar alarm after their house was broken into but it was really a case of locking the stable door after the horse had bolted.*

stacks

stacks of (something) *(informal)* a large amount of (something): *"I don't need any more glasses — I've got stacks of them," said David.*

start

a false start a beginning of an activity which is unsuccessful and so has to be repeated: *Jenny got off to a false start with decorating her bedroom when she hung the first two strips upside down.*

get off to a flying start to have a very successful beginning: *The new girl at work has got off to a flying start by arranging a successful marketing deal.*

state

get into a state to become upset: *It's only a short essay that you have to do; there's no need to get into a state about it.*

steam

run out of steam no longer to have as much energy, enthusiasm, etc as one did: *Rona and Millie were very keen to start their own dressmaking business, but they seem to have run out of steam.*

steer

steer clear of (someone/something) to avoid contact with (someone or something): *We're all steering clear of Petra — she's looking for volunteers to deliver leaflets.*

stretch

at full stretch exerting full power, energy, etc in doing something: *I would like to help you with your garden, but I am already at full stretch doing my household chores.*

strike

strike it lucky to have good luck in a particular matter: *I do not know what to expect when I go on holiday but I hope to strike it lucky and find good beaches.*

strings

pull strings to use personal influence or power to gain some kind of advantage: *Dick's father might have pulled a few strings to get him a job in the law firm — he's a judge.*

stroke

not to do a stroke to do no work whatsoever: *Dad's paying my brother to look after the garden but so far he hasn't done a stroke.*

OPPOSITE

work one's fingers to the bone to work extremely hard: *The couple had ten children and had to work their fingers to the bone in order to feed and clothe them.*

stuff

do one's stuff *(informal)* to perform in the expected way, to show one's abilities: *When the singer took to the stage and did her stuff, the crowd cheered.*

suit

follow suit to do what someone else has just done: *Jack left the room and his friends followed suit.*

surface

scratch the surface to deal with only a very small part of a problem, subject, etc: *Jane lent me some money to pay my debts but the loan barely scratched the surface of my financial problems.*

sweat

be in a cold sweat to be in a state of fear and anxiety: *The girls were in a cold sweat waiting to see if the last bus had gone.*

sweat it out *(informal)* to endure a difficult situation: *My manager at work is really difficult to get on with but I've decided to sweat it out and hope that I can find a new job next year.*

swing

in full swing going ahead busily or vigorously: *The party was in full swing when I arrived.*

swords

cross swords with (someone) to quarrel with (someone), to have a disagreement with (someone): *The president of the tennis club is not used to people disagreeing with him but the new member has crossed swords with him over the membership rules.*

tail

turn tail to run away: *I wanted to turn tail when it was my turn to be interviewed.*

SIMILAR

take to one's heels: to run away: *The burglars took to their heels when they saw the police car.*

take

do a double take to look at, or think about, someone or something a second time, as a result of not having seen or understood properly the first time: *Paul did a double take when Susan walked in with her sister as he did not know that she had a twin.*

take it/things easy not to work, etc hard or energetically: *Richard had been over-working and was told to take things easy for a while.*

SIMILAR

sit back to take a rest: *You've done all the cooking — now sit back and let us do the washing-up.*

taken

be taken with (someone/something) to think that someone or something is very pleasing or attractive: *Jane seems to be very taken with her new boyfriend.*

tape

red tape annoying and unnecessarily strict rules and regulations: *It would be much quicker if you could cut through the red tape and just give me my passport.*

teeth

armed to the teeth fully armed with the weapons, tools, information, etc required: *I was babysitting last night so I went armed to the teeth with nappies, rattles and toys.*

in the teeth of (something) against or in the opposition to (something): *John decided to leave school in the teeth of his parents' disapproval.*

tenterhooks

on tenterhooks uncertain and extremely tense and nervous about what is going to happen: *The exam results were to be announced and the students were on tenterhooks.*

thing

a near thing the state or act of having narrowly avoided an accident or punishment: *Stan should drive more carefully — that was a near thing when he overtook that lorry.*

have a good thing going to have arranged a very pleasant or rewarding position, relationship, etc. *I thought about looking for a new job but then I realized that I have a good thing going where I am.*

to do things by halves (usually in negative statements) to do things in a careless way: *My mother does not do things by halves and my sister's wedding was a lavish event.*

ticking-off

give (someone) a ticking-off to scold (someone), usually mildly: *The manager gave Shona a ticking-off for leaving work early.*

tied

be tied up to be busy, to be occupied with something: *I can't spare the time to come to lunch — I'll be tied up with meetings all morning.*

time

have done one's time to have served a prison sentence, to have paid the price for committing a wrongful act: *Henry has done his time and we should forgive him and let him start a new life.*

have no time for (someone/something) to despise (someone or something): *Pauline has no time for lawyers after she spent all that money getting divorced.*

have the time of one's life to enjoy oneself very much: *Thank you so much for asking me to come to the party — I had the time of my life.*

have time on one's hands to have a great deal of free time: *Sheila has a lot of time on her hands now that her children have all grown up.*

OPPOSITE

have one's hands full to be very busy, to have a great many things to do: *Jane has her hands full with a part-time job and three children to look after.*

play for time to delay a decision or action to see if conditions improve: *I'm playing for time — I'm not accepting the job which I've been offered until I know if I'm getting a substantial pay rise at my present firm.*

tools

down tools to stop working, sometimes suddenly: *We were working in the garden, but it was so hot that we decided to down tools and go for a drink. One of the workers was sacked and the others downed tools and went on strike.*

tooth

fight tooth and nail to fight fiercely and with all one's strength: *I'll fight tooth and nail to stop them from sending granny home from hospital before she is better.*

top

over the top *(informal)* too much, excessive *I know you are angry, but I think that hitting the child is over the top.*

touch

lose touch with (someone) to stop communicating with (someone): *Rachel and Leo used to be very good friends, but they lost touch with each other when they left university.*

town

paint the town/paint the town red to celebrate by going out to enjoy oneself in an extravagant, often noisy manner: *When the local football team won the cup all the fans decided to paint the town red.*

SIMILAR

live it up *(informal)* to enjoy oneself in an extravagant, often noisy manner: *The students plan to live it up as soon as they finish their exams.*

tree

up a gum tree *(informal)* in a hopeless situation: *If I can't find the key for the front door I'm really going to be up a gum tree.*

trick

never miss a trick never to miss an opportunity to gain some advantage or profit: *I'm not surprised that Jane's mother has made a lot of money from investing in the new computer games firm — she's never misses a trick.*

trolley

off one's trolley *(informal)* insane, very foolish: *You must be off your trolley if you think that I'm going to buy that car from you; it's a total wreck!*

troubles

teething troubles problems or difficulties which occur at the start of something: *The builders had a few teething troubles with our new office block but they finished it on schedule.*

trumpet

blow one's own trumpet to boast , to praise oneself greatly: *You may have won the race but there is no need to blow your own trumpet.*

trumps

turn up trumps to behave well or to do the right thing, especially unexpectedly: *John has a reputation for being mean, but he turned up trumps when he lent us money for the deposit on our flat.*

tune

change one's tune to change one's mind, opinions or attitude: *You've changed your tune about the film since speaking to Paul.*

SIMILAR

shift one's ground to change one's mind or opinions: *We tried to persuade Vera that she was being too critical of Mark, but she refused to shift her ground.*

turn

one good turn deserves another if someone does one a favour one should do that person a favour in return: *There's no need to pay me for fixing your washing machine — you put up those shelves for me and one good turn deserves another.*

turn (somewhere) upside down to cause confusion and mess (somewhere), usually when looking thoroughly for something: *The police turned the students' flat upside down looking for drugs. I've turned the place upside down and I can't find my ring.*

two

put two and two together to work out something: *It took me a long time but I finally put two and two together.*

umbrage

take umbrage to feel and show that one is offended at something that someone else has done: *I took umbrage at the way that the others decided what film we were going to see without even asking my opinion.*

SIMILAR

take the huff *(informal)* to become sulky or silent because one feels offended or displeased about something: *Moira took the huff when we went to the cinema without asking her to come along.*

up

be on the up and up *(informal)* to be doing very well, especially financially: *Things have been on the up and up for Simon since he took that job at the bank.*

OPPOSITE

go downhill to get worse, to deteriorate: *The firm was once very successful, but it's been going downhill recently.*

what's up with (someone/something)? what is wrong with someone or something?: *What's up with Julie — I just saw her running down the road crying?*

U-turn

do a U-turn to change completely a decision, attitude, etc: *The union agreed to the pay rise at first but then did a U-turn and refused to accept management's offer.*

variety

variety is the spice of life many different things can happen in life but the changes that one experiences are what makes it interesting: *Bob is taking me to a Mexican restaurant tonight — I don't know if I will like it but variety is the spice of life, after all.*

veil

draw a veil over (something) not to discuss or mention (something) in the belief that it is better forgotten: *Philip used to be married but he tends to draw a veil over that.*

victory

a landslide victory an election victory won by a very large number of votes: *The Prime Minister was delighted that he had proved his critics wrong and the general election had been a landslide victory for his party.*

villain

the villain of the piece the person responsible for doing something wrong: *It turned out that Tom was the villain of the piece because he had lost the map.*

voice

lose one's voice to be unable to speak because of having a sore throat, etc: *I could not join in the singing at the party because I lost my voice.*

walk

walk it to win or succeed easily: *I have an exam tomorrow but I've done so much work that I expect to walk it.*

wall

go to the wall to fail, to be financially unsuccessful, to go bankrupt: *Sales of the new product were poor and the company went to the wall.*

SIMILAR

go bust (informal) to fail financially, to go bankrupt: *Jim started his firm without enough capital and he's gone bust.*

off the wall (informal) strange, weird: *I don't understand Chris — some of her comments are completely off the wall.*

wars

have been in the wars to have suffered slight injury in the course of a rough activity: *Joseph came home from school last night with his coat all torn — he looked as if he had been in the wars.*

water

in hot water in trouble: *You'll be in hot water if you're late for work again.*

SIMILAR

in the soup (informal) in trouble: *Tom is really in the soup — the police caught him driving without a licence.*

throw/pour cold water on (something) to be very discouraging about (something): *We had great fun making holiday plans and then Sid threw cold water on them by reminding us that we had no money!*

waterloo

meet our Waterloo to be finally defeated: *'It's time to meet our Waterloo,' said the captain of the team as they went out on the pitch to play the champions.*

make waves to cause trouble: *This was a very peaceful place to work until Tom arrived — he's always making waves.*

OPPOSITE

pour oil on troubled waters to try to bring peace and calm to a violent situation, angry person, etc: *My two friends are always arguing and I am left to pour oil on troubled waters.*

way

learn the hard way to learn from one's own experiences (often unpleasant): *Susan learnt the hard way that she had to spend more time studying if she wanted to pass her exams.*

pave the way for (something) to make it possible for (something) to happen: *The new school rules pave the way for the students to play a part in the running of the school.*

pay one's way to pay for one's own expenses: *I like having a job and being able to pay my way.*

pick one's way to go carefully: *We had to pick our way through broken glass to get to our front door.*

rub (someone) up the wrong way to annoy (someone): *I don't get on with Mike — he always manages to rub me up the wrong way.*

stand in (someone's/something's) way to prevent (someone) from doing something or to prevent (something) from happening, to obstruct (someone or something): *If our daughter wants to go to drama school we won't stand in her way although it is difficult to get work in the theatre. The trade unions say that they will not stand in the way of technological advancement.*

weakness

have a weakness for (someone/something) to have a liking for someone or something: *Debbie is trying to lose weight, but is finding it difficult because she has a weakness for chocolate.*

weather

make heavy weather of (something) to find great difficulty in doing something that should be easy: *The teacher thought that the essay topic was very simple and could not understand why the students seemed to be making such heavy weather of it.*

OPPOSITE

do (something) with both hands tied behind one's back to do (something) very easily: *My father could solve these maths problems with both hands tied behind his back.*

under the weather unwell: *Kate's a bit under the weather — she thinks she's getting flu.*

OPPOSITE
hale and hearty extremely healthy: *Everyone else has a cold but Harry is looking hale and hearty.*

weaving

get weaving (*informal*) to start moving or working quickly: *You had better get weaving if you want to get that essay finished for tomorrow.*

SIMILAR
get cracking (*informal*) to start moving or working quickly: *We'd better get cracking or we will miss the bus.*

weight

pull one's weight to do one's share of a task: *We have to get all these books packed up by tonight and so we'll all have to pull our weight.*

SIMILAR
do one's bit to do one's share of a task: *Mother doesn't do all the housework — all the family members have to do their bit.*

well

the well has run dry there is nothing left in what was formerly a plentiful source of something: *The local bookshop used to be a good place to buy antiquarian books, but it became very popular with tourists, and now the well has run dry.*

whip

crack the whip to behave in a very strict way: *The teacher cracked the whip and told the class to behave or she would make them stay late.*

whistle

blow the whistle on (someone) to report or make public (someone's) dishonest or illegal activities: *No-one knew who broke the window until Charlie blew the whistle on Patrick.*

willies

give (someone) the willies (*informal*) to make (someone) feel nervous and afraid: *That man that was staring at me really gave me the willies.*

SIMILAR
give (someone) the creeps (*informal*) to make (someone) feel nervous and afraid, to disgust (someone): *I don't like the way that man looked at me — he gave me the creeps.*

wind

like the wind very quickly: *The child ran like the wind to tell his mother the good news.*

OPPOSITE
at a snail's space very slowly: *The roads were busy and all the cars were moving at a snail's pace.*

put the wind up (someone) to cause (someone) to be concerned or anxious: *The manager really put the wind up Lesley when she told her that if she was late again she would get the sack.*

sail close to the wind to engage in activities which are not illegal but which come close to being so: *Some of the local traders sail close to the wind although they have never been found guilty of selling stolen goods.*

OPPOSITE
be on the level (*informal*) to be honest and act lawfully: *Quite a few second-hand car salesmen are not on the level these days.*

wings

spread one's wings to do things that are more ambitious or adventurous than one has been doing before: *Greg has been in the same job in the same small town all his life, and he now wants to spread his wings and move to the city.*

wink

not to sleep a wink to be unable to sleep: *I could not sleep a wink last night for worrying about my interview.*

OPPOSITE
sleep like a log to sleep very deeply: *After the long journey I slept like a log.*

wits

keep one's wits about one to be careful and alert: *If you are going to walk home through the park remember to keep your wits about you.*

SIMILAR
watch one's step to be careful and cautious: You had better watch your step if you join that department because the manager is very strict.

scare/frighten (someone) out of (his/her) wits to frighten (someone) very much: *We were frightened out of our wits when we heard the strange noise coming from the graveyard.*

SIMILAR

frighten (someone) to death to make (someone) extremely frightened: *You frightened me to death creeping up behind me like that.*

woman

scarlet woman an extremely immoral woman: *Dave's mother treats Jill like a scarlet woman just because she's divorced.*

wonders

wonders will never cease used to describe a situation which is very unusual and surprising: *Sheila was early for work today — wonders will never cease!*

wool

pull the wool over (someone's) eyes to deceive (someone): *He tried to pull the wool over my eyes, but I knew that he was lying.*

word

from the word go from the very start: *From the word go I knew that I was not going to get on with my new flat-mate.*

take (someone's) word for it to believe what someone says without question: *I have not read the book, but I will take your word for it that dad will like it.*

work

have one's work cut out to face a difficult task: *Julie will have her work cut out when the baby is born.*

world

be dead to the world to be deeply asleep: *I thought that I heard the baby cry but he was dead to the world.*

do (someone) the world of good to have a very good effect on (someone), to be of great benefit to (someone): *Olive has been ill — a week's holiday in the sun will do her the world of good.*

think the world of (someone) to be very fond of (someone): *Jill thought the world of her daughter-in-law and was very upset when her son divorced her.*

SIMILAR

think there is no-one like (someone) to be extremely fond of (someone), to value (someone) highly: *Clare always goes to her grandmother when she has a problem — she thinks there's no-one like her.*

worried

worried sick extremely anxious and worried: *The family on the beach can't find their little girl and they are worried sick.*

worse

none the worse for (something) to be completely unharmed by something: *Diane fell down the stairs but she was none the worse for her fall.*

wraps

keep (something) under wraps to keep (something) secret: *Howard and Tracey are getting married, but they are keeping it under wraps until they have told their parents. The firm is keeping its new product under wraps until the official launch.*

SIMILAR

keep (something) under one's hat to keep quiet about (something), to keep (something) a secret: *Keep this under your hat but I'm moving to a new job.*

writing

the writing is on the wall a sign that a disaster or failure is about to happen: *Derek realized that the writing was on the wall and that he would have to close down the factory.*

younger

be not getting any younger to be getting older: *Margie doesn't realize that she's not getting any younger and tries to compete with athletes who are much younger and fitter than she is.*

Answers

1. The Driving Test

1 No, you would be feeling nervous.
2 No, you usually get up early in the morning.
3 Luke was surprised that he was left to **foot the bill** in the restaurant — he had thought that they were going to divide it among them.
4 No, you would leave it until a later time.
5 Yes.
6 No, you want it very much.
7 screw up one's courage.
8 a piece of cake.
9 No.
10 grin like a Cheshire cat or be all smiles.

2. Avoiding Party Preparations

1 No, you ignore them.
2 No.
3 You are feeling tired.
4 The robbers are lying low while the police are looking for them.
5 in someone's good books.
6 If you were looking for something.
7 It's time to make myself scarce — my brother has discovered that I got a stain on his best silk tie.
8 in hot water.
9 If someone is very nervous and restless you would say that they are like a cat on hot bricks.
10 Yes.

3. Saving a Business

1 No, you would be looking miserable.
2 in the black.
3 at the beginning of something.
4 get (something) off the ground.
5 The firm is losing sales and the workers are worrying that it will go to the wall.
6 No, it will take some time.
7 Dad will see red if you take his car without permission.
8 You are nervous.
9 No.
10 draw in one's horns.

4. What to Wear

1 No, you have not decided.
2 No.
3 After he was declared redundant the family had to live on a shoestring.
4 There is only one thing which you can do.
5 No.
6 No, they are in a poor state of repair.
7 The two little girls looked like two peas in a pod.
8 No.
9 Mike loves working outdoors — a job as a gardener will suit him to a T.
10 No.

5. A Proposal of Marriage

1 The children were over the moon when they were told of the party.
2 When a man asks a woman to marry him we say that he has popped the question.
3 No.
4 think the world of (someone).
5 No.
6 No.
7 gave the show away.
8 No.
9 Yes.
10 get hitched.

6. Mother's Ban on Motorbikes

1 No.
2 No.
3 at a snail's pace.
4 in a completely different situation.
5 Amy is worried sick because she has lost her job and cannot afford to pay the rent.
6 You'll be dicing with death if you drive that old car.
7 Get out of the burning house now. Don't risk your neck!
8 No.
9 be at each other's throats.
10 No.

7. Amy's Holiday Problem

1 fly off the handle.
2 No.
3 Sue has a new boyfriend — she stopped going steady with Mike last month.
4 No.
5 No.
6 The Smith's youngest daughter has her grandfather wrapped round her little finger.
7 take one's time.
8 No.
9 No.
10 live it up.

8. Finding a Flat-mate

1 I know you're looking for a new secretary but I can't think of anyone who fits the bill.
2 No.
3 The old man is as poor as a church mouse.
4 No.
5 get cracking; step on it.
6 At a pinch we could get eight people round the dining-room table.
7 No.
8 Yes.
9 The patient was very badly injured but the doctors are hoping against hope that he will survive.
10 be a weight off one's mind.

9. Night Fears

1 nervous and scared.
2 We were scared out of our wits when the old man threatened us.
3 chicken out of doing something.
4 Beth had to put a brave face on it when her boyfriend went off with another girl.
5 No.
6 at night.
7 The children went straight to bed and are dead to the world now.
8 Yes.
9 The boy's blood ran cold when he saw the knife in his attacker's hand.
10 No.

10. A Student Joke

1 No.
2 No.
3 No.
4 They are helping you.
5 This novel is as dull as ditchwater.
6 No.
7 You are afraid and anxious.
8 No.
9 laugh one's head off.
10 George's car hadn't really been stolen — his friends were taking the mickey out of him.

11. The End of the Affair

1 No.
2 Yes.
3 Kim and Roy have had a serious quarrel but they have decided to bury the hatchet.
4 The hockey team was playing very well but it now seems to have struck a bad patch.
5 No.

6 The neighbours were obviously feeling annoyed about the parking problems caused by the new pub and so the pub owner called a meeting to try to clear the air.
7 No.
8 The business is losing money and the owners have decided to call it a day and close the shop.
9 Tom and Sheila have decided that their marriage has come to the end of the road and have decided to get a divorce.
10 There are plenty more pebbles on the beach.

12. Getting the Girl

1 He likes her very much.
2 grasp the nettle.
3 Ted is quite a good chess player but he's not in the same league as the winner of the tournament.
4 No.
5 welcome someone with open arms.
6 No.
7 Jock is determined not to join the football team and I don't think you'll be able to twist his arm.
8 No.
9 The workers agreed to strike but some of them changed their minds and their colleagues thought that they had sold them down the river.
10 No.

13. Shop-keeping

1 No.
2 morning
3 No.
4 hale and hearty.
5 The new teacher seems very stern but she has her heart in the right place — she was kind to little Susie when she lost her lunch money.
6 as fast as they can.
7 No.
8 The shops were full of customers on Christmas Eve and the shop assistants were rushed off their feet.
9 No.
10 No.

14. Work Experience

1 It is Bert's final year and he is having to keep his nose to the grindstone.
2 do one's bit.
3 No.
4 The sweater which your aunt gave you is not fashionable but you should not look a gift horse in the mouth.
5 No.
6 No.
7 It has a bad effect.

8 Matt's father is president of the cricket club and, if you want to become a member, he could pull strings.
9 No.
10 No.

15. A Drive in the Country
1 I'm going for a stroll along the beach to blow the cobwebs away.
2 No.
3 No.
4 No.
5 Fay's father is paying for the trip and he is insisting on calling the shots.
6 We don't have a fixed route for our holiday in England — we're just playing it by ear.
7 No.
8 No.
9 It was such an easy job but the young gardener made heavy weather of it.
10 No.

16. A Reluctant Model
1 I've been roped in to sell tickets for the college dance but I really don't want to.
2 be at a loose end.
3 I knew that Rita wouldn't take no for an answer and so I took the line of least resistance.
4 I'm getting out of here — I don't want Rob bending my hear about football all evening.
5 No.
6 I was going to clean the kitchen before my mother arrived, but she caught me on the hop with dirty dishes in the sink.
7 stay put.
8 No, they stop working.
9 I had difficulty in standing up as my foot had gone to sleep.
10 Wild horses wouldn't get me to go up in a hot-air balloon.

17. A Party is Planned
1 Yes.
2 Jean's looking for a green tablecloth — do you think this fits the bill?
3 The teacher should be encouraging the students but she seems to throw cold water on all their ideas.
4 put a damper on something.
5 The goalkeeper broke his leg and it cast a shadow over our team's victory.
6 No.
7 untidy.
8 Janet and Mark are going to put their heads together to try to find a solution to the noise problem.

9 We had planned to borrow my parents' caravan for our holiday but my dad threw a spanner in the works by saying that he had just sold it.
10 No.

18. Which University?
1 No.
2 Her parents hope that Tracy will soon come out of her shell — she's so shy that she won't talk to anyone.
3 Frank wants to work overseas — he's tired of working on the family farm and wants to spread his wings.
4 Charlie is 35 years old and still lives with his mother — he must be tied to her apron-strings.
5 No.
6 No.
7 Moving to a new house will do the family the world of good.
8 When students go to university they rub shoulders with people from many different backgrounds.
9 No.
10 No.

19. Attending an Auction
1 try one's hand at something.
2 No.
3 No.
4 No.
5 If Frankie had been on the ball he would have applied for a grant to fund his research project.
6 No.
7 We were not surprised that Ralph ended up in prison — he always sailed close to the wind.
8 No.
9 Trust Jim to find out about the free concert — he never misses a trick.
10 No.

20. Election for President
1 No.
2 No.
3 No.
4 Lucy is hoping to run the marathon next year but she does not have the ghost of a chance of winning it.
5 No.
6 Tracy does not like her doctor, but she is not going to move to another one until after the baby is born, as she does not think it is a good idea to change horses in mid-stream.
7 Yes.
8 No.
9 Vicky was on edge as she walked down the dark, lonely road.
10 No.

21. Buying a Car
1 You do care.
2 No.
3 Steve said that the car usually went like a dream and he could not understand why it would not start.
4 No.
5 No, he is someone who questions everything.
6 No.
7 Don't buy a bike from him — he sold me a pup last year.
8 Yes.
9 No.
10 I tried to tell him not to speed but he had to learn the hard way.

22. Nearly a Disaster
1 No.
2 No, he is expected to do very well.
3 David was embarrassed when the boss told him to stop playing the fool during meetings.
4 No.
5 'I have a feeling that I'm about to meet my Waterloo,' said Lesley as she walked on to the tennis court.
6 No.
7 Yes.
8 get the red light.
9 No.
10 three times.

23. An Unwelcome Friend Returns
1 No.
2 be inside.
3 No.
4 John said that he will not steal again, but I think I will take that with a pinch of salt.
5 No.
6 'I would like to help you but it was your mistake and you will have to carry the can this time,' said Bob's mother.
7 No.
8 Jean hopes that she will not lose touch with her brother when he moves to Australia.
9 Peter and Sharon used to go out with each other before they went away to university, and now that they have both come home they are hoping that they can pick up where they left off.
10 No.

24. An Anniversary Dinner
1 No.
2 It's expensive.
3 Yes, you have enough and more.
4 Yes.

5 pull one's weight.
6 Sylvia wanted to start her own business, but she did not want to bite off more than she could chew.
7 You like it.
8 No.
9 Joseph decided to clear the decks before he began to fix the broken shelf.
10 No.

25. A Marathon
1 No.
2 No.
3 James came within an ace of winning the gold medal.
4 Yes.
5 I'm looking forward to making my presentation to the class — it gives me a chance to give a good account of myself.
6 No.
7 No.
8 We are hoping to have a barbecue on Saturday but it depends on the weather and that is in the lap of the gods.
9 No.
10 No.

26. Amateur Decorators
1 No.
2 I would like to help you put up the shelves but I'm all fingers and thumbs today.
3 No.
4 Studying for exams at school is one thing but when you get to university it's a different ball game.
5 No.
6 like gold dust.
7 I know that you are disappointed that you failed your exam but you need to get your act together and start studying for the next one.
8 John was working in the newsagent but he asked if I could hold the fort while he went out for lunch.
9 No.
10 No.

27. A Case of Mistaken Identity
1 have one's hands full.
2 I am suspicious about the boy who is waiting at the bus stop — I'm sure that he's up to no good.
3 No.
4 Yes.
5 Melanie slapped Pam for ruining her book and I think that her action was over the top.
6 No.
7 No.
8 No.

9 Oliver cooked his goose when he was rude to his grandmother — she has not left him anything in her will.

10 No.

28. Deceiving the Boss

1 No.

2 look as though one has stepped out of a bandbox.

3 The boss gave Bob his marching orders after he was late for the third day in a row.

4 No.

5 William said that he would fix my washing machine but he is all mouth and trousers.

6 No.

7 If you play your cards right Jill might agree to go out with you.

8 No.

9 No.

10 No, it is very effective.

29. Unsuccessful Entertainers

1 No.

2 have a stab at.

3 No.

4 No.

5 I want to ask my boss for a raise but I think I will see how the land lies.

6 No.

7 No.

8 No.

9 Could you please make less noise? If I have to shout any more I will lose my voice.

10 No.

30. A Missing Boat

1 be on cloud nine.

2 John has been studying very hard for his exams. I think he is determined to make a go of it this time.

3 No.

4 I'm really happy to be moving to London but the only fly in the ointment is that I will have to sell my house.

5 No.

6 No, you are very upset.

7 No, you are very angry.

8 I'm sorry that the eggs got broken when I dropped your bag but accidents will happen.

9 No.

10 I'm only one hour later than I said I would be — keep your hair on!

31. Opening a Sandwich Bar

1 Don't put the cart before the horse. I think you should get to know him better before you think about getting married.

2 take one's time

3 Yes, you are very annoyed.

4 No.

5 No.

6 I felt like the villain of the piece when Lynne pointed out that I had forgotten to pass on the message.

7 No.

8 No.

9 No.

10 I am upset that Jamie was unfaithful, but I may as well chalk it up to experience.

32. Toothache

1 No.

2 give someone the creeps.

3 No.

4 Frank kept telling me that lots of people fail university exams — but he's just a Job's comforter.

5 No.

6 No.

7 I told him that it was out of my control — you can take a horse to the water but you can't make it drink.

8 No.

9 No.

10 No.

33. A Protest Movement

1 No.

2 make someone's hackles rise.

3 Yes.

4 James fought tooth and nail to stay in his house when his landlord tried to evict him.

5 No.

6 The soldiers were armed to the teeth and ready to take on the enemy.

7 No.

8 No.

9 There is a lot of red tape to sort out before you can get married.

10 No.

34. Feuding Friends

1 No.

2 No.

3 No.

4 The issue of getting married has always been a bone of contention for Jane and Peter.

5 No.

6 rattle someone's cage.

7 I used to fight with my brother all the time — my mum was always having to pour oil on troubled waters.

8 No.

9 I'll get you to finish that essay even if I have to hold a pistol to your head.

10 No.

35. Job-hunting

1 No.
2 No.
3 No.
4 When I saw the black shape in the graveyard it really made my hair stand on end.
5 No.
6 I'm not afraid to call a spade a spade and I say that he is a liar.
7 No.
8 sober as a judge.
9 I'm worried about George — since he lost his job he's really been hitting the bottle.
10 I'm so depressed after failing my exams that I'm just going to go home and drown my sorrows.

36. No longer a Student

1 No.
2 I think that you should apply to the other college too and not put all your eggs in one basket.
3 stand on one's own (two) feet.
4 Don't hedge your bets — just say which dress you prefer.
5 No.
6 The holiday went by the board when John lost his job.
7 No.
8 No.
9 No.
10 No.

37. Holiday Disagreement

1 No.
2 No.
3 My driving lessons have been going really well recently — I think I'll strike while the iron is hot and apply to do my test.
4 My boss seems to be very pleasant but it's a case of the iron hand in the velvet glove.
5 Yes.
6 Yes.
7 do a U-turn
8 Dave and Jane have decided to get married in the teeth of her parents' disapproval.
9 Yes.
10 You are so lucky to be offered that job — if I were you I would jump at the chance.

38. Looking for a Corpse

1 Yes.
2 in the soup.
3 The doctor looked in her bag of tricks and brought out some cough medicine.
4 No.
5 No.
6 If you keep practising skating you will soon get the hang of it.
7 No.
8 It may go against the grain but I think you should apologize.
9 If you want to beat Fred at chess you will have to keep your wits about you.
10 No.

39. Flat-hunting

1 No.
2 No.
3 Yes.
4 I think that I will get my lawyer to give the contract the once-over before I sign it.
5 get cracking.
6 Yes.
7 The garden is in a bit of a mess but I'll soon lick it into shape.
8 Yes.
9 No.
10 Angela intends to get her pound of flesh when they get divorced.

40. A Jumble Sale

1 No.
2 I think that I should start looking for another job — I have a feeling that my days are numbered at the bookshop.
3 a drop in the ocean.
4 No.
5 The bank manager refused to give Andy a loan because he thought that he was already at full stretch with his mortgage.
6 No.
7 The rowing team got off to a flying start but ran out of energy at the end of the race.
8 I will ask the architect to look at the plans since she has a nose for design faults.
9 No.
10 No.

41. A Visit to the Gym

1 eat like a horse.
2 Yes.
3 I've asked the whole class to come to the wedding — the more the merrier.
4 My father never does things by halves — at the barbecue he made enough food to feed an army.
5 Yes.
6 No.
7 Yes.
8 I feel as fresh as a daisy after that nap.

9 I know that Harold said that everything would be all right but I can't help feeling that I've been lulled into a false sense of security.

10 No.

42. A Reluctant Shopper

1 No.

2 No.

3 Jack's putting a brave face on it but I think that he is really unhappy in his new job.

4 No.

5 No.

6 I was trying to get in touch with Helen all week and I eventually ran her to earth in the library.

7 Yes.

8 I think that there must have been an accident since the High Street is crawling with police and I saw three ambulances.

9 No.

10 have the patience of a saint.

43. A New Session

1 No.

2 No.

3 make a pig's ear of something.

4 I don't have any sympathy for the boy who got sent to prison for stealing cars — he's made his bed and now he must lie on it.

5 No, you have tried very hard.

6 Steve is taking his wife on a cruise because he thinks she deserves a final fling before going back to work full time.

7 I feel sorry for the next captain of the team — Jim was very popular and he will be a hard act to follow.

8 You admit defeat.

9 No.

10 No, you have a thorough knowledge of it.

44. Out goes the Boss

1 No.

2 No.

3 Tom had better be careful that the tax department does not find out about his undeclared earnings — he's been on the fiddle for years.

4 have it in for someone.

5 Yes.

6 No.

7 Yes.

8 The burning question is will Sarah say yes to Roger's proposal.

9 No.

10 No.

45. Dancing Lessons

1 No.

2 No.

3 The opening of the supermarket sealed the fate of several small shops in the village.

4 No.

5 No.

6 I'm going to help Sam decorate his flat because he fixed my car for me last week and one good turn deserves another.

7 No.

8 No.

9 Debbie bought her a new pair of shoes to wear to the ball because her new dress looked so lovely that she felt it would be a shame to spoil the ship for a hap'orth o' tar.

10 No.

46. To Retire or Not to Retire

1 sit back.

2 You shouldn't look after that huge garden by yourself — you're not getting any younger.

3 No, you are nearly 30 years old.

4 Jane apologized for not coming to the party, saying that she has not had a moment to call her own since she had the baby.

5 No.

6 Yes.

7 No.

8 No.

9 No.

10 No.

47. Waiting for Results

1 No.

2 No.

3 No.

4 John should get charged for assaulting Bob and I'm going to make it my business to see that he does.

5 No.

6 The football coach told the team to keep their chins up and try to play better in the second half.

7 No.

8 Yes.

9 Helen is finding the work at university really difficult but she has decided to sweat it out until the end of her first year at least.

10 No.

48. An Allergic Reaction

1 No.

2 No.

3 yes.

4 It was a lovely holiday — the weather was great and we felt at home in the hotel.
5 Everyone was delighted when Sarah got up and started doing her stuff on the dance floor.
6 No.
7 Yes.
8 Alex says he's at death's door, but he's only suffering from a hangover.
9 Yes.
10 Yes.

49. A Missing Child
1 No.
2 Lisa was as white as a sheet after she crashed her car into the wall.
3 The villagers had a meeting at the town hall and agreed that they would all rally round to raise funds to fix the church roof.
4 be at the helm.
5 No.
6 I find it very difficult to concentrate on driving when Roger is breathing down my neck and telling me that I am going too slowly.
7 No.
8 No.
9 I have not had my results back yet, but I was talking to my tutor yesterday and, reading between the lines, I think that I've got a really good mark for my essay.
10 No.

50. Up a Tree
1 No.
2 Yes.
3 Yvonne is so fickle, she was all over Bob at the party, but she totally ignored him when she saw him in the street the next day.
4 a knight in shining armour.
5 No.
6 No.
7 No.
8 If you are getting a lift from Adam you will have to hang on like grim death because he always drives too fast.
9 Dawn was very quick off the mark when I told her that there was a reward for the person who finished the work first.
10 Yes.

51.Exam Nerves
1 Yes.
2 No.
3 Julie has left her husband after finding out that he was having an affair and I'm glad his chicken's have come home to roost.

4 Helen said that I was a terrible cook but that's the pot calling the kettle black, because everything she makes tastes burnt.
5 No.
6 No.
7 in hot water.
8 No.
9 No, you do have a problem in understanding it.
10 We had given up trying to get a package holiday to Europe that we could afford when the travel agent pulled a rabbit out of a hat.

52. Misery at Work
1 separate the wheat from the chaff.
2 No.
3 No.
4 Maureen did not want to make a presentation to the whole class because she was terrified of falling flat on her face.
5 No.
6 Yes.
7 Tom offered me a job in his butcher's shop, but I would sooner run a mile than work there — I'm a vegetarian!
8 No.
9 I asked john not to drink too much at the party but somehow I feel that I was wasting my breath.
10 No.

53. A Riding Lesson
1 No.
2 No, you are extremely interested in it.
3 No.
4 Mrs Williams is a leading light in the local theatrical company — they never put on a show without her.
5 Yes.
6 Colin has decided to leave university and we all think that he has taken leave of his senses.
7 No.
8 No.
9 I've agreed to go skating with Jane on Saturday but I can't help feeling that I'm taking my life in my hands.
10 One of my friends has scratched the driver's door and that's put the lid on the chances of Dad lending me the car ever again.

54. Dog-minding
1 Yes.
2 take the huff.
3 No.
4 Yes.
5 Dad has just noticed that the window is broken — the fat is in the fire now.
6 make a clean breast about something.

7 Susan could not believe that her husband had been having an affair right under her very nose.

8 No.

9 The child led his mother a merry dance by having a different favourite food each day.

10 I can't believe that John is the person who has been stealing from us — he looks as though butter wouldn't melt in his mouth.

55. Market Research

1 on the stocks.

2 Yes.

3 Jane was meant to be babysitting for me tonight but she just phoned and cancelled and so I'm really left in the lurch.

4 Fraser had the brass neck to phone and ask if he could get his job back after being fired for stealing.

5 Yes.

6 Yes.

7 No.

8 I know that I'm late but there is no need to bite my head off.

9 Yes.

10 Betty was really happy when she received the flowers — they really made her day.

56. A Wrong Diagnosis

1 The food is delicious but I cannot quite put my finger on what herbs you have used.

2 Yes.

3 No.

4 You will have the devil of a job getting tickets for that concert.

5 No.

6 No.

7 Yes.

8 I put two and two together and realized that john had stolen the money.

9 spot on.

10 No, you do know what will happen and you are confident of success.

57. Essay Time

1 No.

2 No.

3 Yes.

4 I hope that you have a change of heart and decide to go to the hospital appointment.

5 Have I enough money to buy a flat? That will be the day!

6 No.

7 No.

8 I don't want to tempt fate by choosing a name for the baby before it is born.

9 I read the article that was in the newspaper but I could not make head nor tail of it.

10 crystal clear.

58. Forming a Band

1 No.

2 No.

3 Yes.

4 Before we make our final decision I have another suggestion that I would like to run up the flagpole.

5 Yes.

6 My boss offered me a raise in a last-ditch effort to make me stay but I had already found another job.

7 No, it fails.

8 No.

9 pass muster.

10 No.